STUFF EVERY
SUSHI LOVER
SHOULD KNOW

STUFF EVERY SUSHI LOVER SHOULD KNOW

Marc Luber and Brett Cohen

QUIRK BOOKS

PHILADELPHIA

Copyright © 2019 by Quirk Productions, Inc.

Library of Congress Cataloging in Publication Number: 2019930330

ISBN: 978-1-68369-158-7

Printed in China

Typeset in Trend Sans, Brandon Grotesque, and Adobe Garamond Pro

Cover design by Elissa Flanigan
Interior design by Molly Rose Murphy
Illustrations by Lucy Engelman
Production management by John J. McGurk

Quirk Books
215 Church Street
Philadelphia, PA 19106
quirkbooks.com

10 9 8 7 6 5 4 3 2 1

To

Jackie, Zach, and Natalie

Randi, Ilivia, and Sawyer

SUSHI AT HOME

INTRODUCTION

Do you remember the first time you ate sushi?

For Marc, it was a friend who took him to Nobu in Las Vegas and ordered his dinner with the all-too-common "trust me" approach. For Brett, it involved passing the sushi counter at a farmer's market week after week until finally deciding to take the plunge. We both regarded the experience as intimidating and ultimately dove in when curiosity overtook doubt, but that initial skepticism quickly turned into a love and fascination for sushi.

Certainly, that love starts with an appreciation for the taste of fresh sushi. With so many options, there's always something new to try or a new way to bring different ingredients together. The health benefits don't hurt either; many sushi fish are high in omega-3 fatty acids, which are believed to promote heart health and help maintain low cholesterol levels. Then there's the social aspect of enjoying sushi with friends. Is there a better dining experience than ordering way too much sushi in a gigantic wooden boat—and somehow devouring the entire thing?

Today, sushi meals are almost a weekly thing for us. We've developed a connection to our local sushi restaurants, where the staff know us by name and are eager for us to try their newest roll. We've shared the experience with our friends and families, enjoying novel items and expanding our knowledge and palates together. During our travels, we've popped into local sushi restaurants to explore the regional flavors or experience the omakase. With the proliferation of sushi restaurants and options, there's always something different to try.

That's the great thing about sushi. What started as a means of preserving fish has evolved into an entire style of cuisine available in supermarkets, mall food courts, sushi bars, and high-end restaurants around the world. Its history dates back hundreds of years, with widespread globalization happening in just the last few decades. Each generation sees up-and-coming chefs experimenting with ingredients and introducing unexpected flavors to the cuisine.

We set out to write this book from the fan's perspective by incorporating our own experiences and knowledge with the expertise of the sushi chefs and resources we consulted. We learned a few things along the way and we're certain that you will, too. This book will explore the nuance and customs of the traditional Japanese sushi experience, as well as the modern take on a cuisine that continues to evolve with each generation. We will discover sushi's rich and unique history, provide insight into various menu items, offer recipes for making sushi at home, and so much more—all in the hopes of making the sushi experience more accessible and your approach more aspirational.

Sushi truly is a great adventure. There is so much to explore, with unusual flavors and experiences awaiting at each destination. This book will help you on your journey. So pay attention . . . this stuff is important.

SUSHI
BASICS

WHAT IS SUSHI?

The word *sushi* derives from the Japanese words *su*, meaning vinegar, and *meshi*, meaning rice. Today we use the term to encompass a variety of dishes that are made with fish, vegetables, and rice. Many people think of raw fish as sushi's defining characteristic, but in reality it's all about the rice. (Be sure to share that fact with your vegetarian friends!)

Although sushi has become so popular and ubiquitous that you can find it across the world—and in some cities, on every block—there's an art to sushi, and chefs take personal pride in creating it. This philosophical approach and aesthetic is called *wabi-sabi*, which is all about finding beauty in transience and imperfection.

Today *wabi-sabi* means "wisdom in natural simplicity." The phrase has been used to describe artistic practices in Japanese culture like *hanami* (cherry blossom viewing), *ikebana* (flower arranging), *haiku* (a traditional Japanese poetic form), *bonsai* (cultivating small trees in containers), and, of course, sushi.

A BRIEF HISTORY OF SUSHI

People have been consuming fish and rice for thousands of years, though not always in the same bite. Here are some landmark dates in the development of sushi.

Ca. 1000 BCE–300 CE: Wet-field rice cultivation takes off in southeast Asia, kicking off an agricultural revolution and turning rice into the region's most important crop.

Ca. 100–200: Southeast Asians and the Chinese use lacto-fermentation to preserve fish in rice after it has been scaled, gutted, and packed in salt for months. The result is the earliest form of *narezushi*, or "aged sushi," which is first described in a fourth-century Chinese dictionary. The fish can be stored for many months without spoiling. When it's ready to be eaten, the rice is discarded.

Ca. 700–900: As lacto-fermentation spreads from China to Japan and Buddhists turn to fish in general, and sushi in particular, as a dietary staple, *narezushi* becomes popular.

Ca. 1000–1300s: Golden carp from Lake Biwa, Japan's largest freshwater source, is packed under salted rice for six months to create *funazushi*. Only the wealthiest citizens can afford to eat it.

Ca. 1400s: During a civil war, the Japanese adapt *narezushi* into *namanare* (meaning "fresh fermented"), which reduces the fermentation time from six months to one month. It consists of partly raw fish that is wrapped in rice and consumed fresh. The rice is part of the dish and is no longer thrown out. *Namanare* becomes the most popular type of sushi during the Muromachi period.

1600s: The production of rice vinegar increases in Japan. Matsumoto Yoshiichi, a doctor, began to season sushi rice with rice vinegar, making the fish more tender and flavorful while also cutting the fermentation time down even further, to about 24 hours. This method is developed by sushi makers in the new capital of Edo (the former name of Tokyo) and becomes popular with the rising merchant class.

1700s: Nori seaweed is first pressed into sheets. This development allows for the creation and rise of *makizushi*, or rolled sushi, and makes possible a proliferation of creative combinations of ingredients and cuisine fusions that are the hallmark of modern sushi restaurants.

1820s: Yohei Hanaya, a Japanese sushi maker, evolves the sushi-making process by placing a piece of fresh fish on top of an oblong ball of seasoned rice. Hanaya serves his creations from a sushi stall in the Ryogoku district near the Sumida River, and it becomes wildly popular with travelers who love the "fast food" option for its beauty, fresh flavor, and ease of consumption. Today, this is known as *nigiri* or *edo-mae*, but Hanaya's version was a little different; the fish was slightly cooked or marinated in soy sauce or vinegar to prevent spoilage, and the rice ball was nearly double the size of today's nigiri.

1906: The first sushi restaurant in the United States opens in the Little Tokyo neighborhood of Los Angeles, as a result of Japanese migrants and dignitaries introducing sushi to other cultures during their travels.

1920s: After the Great Kanto Earthquake of 1923, land in Tokyo becomes prohibitively expensive. Sushi vendors migrate indoors and establish *sushi-ya*, or restaurants that specialize in sushi. Around this time, Japanese sushi makers start to create rules and customs for preparation and consumption, transforming the changes local opinions of the ingredient and, in the process, makes salmon a staple in sushi restaurants around the world.

2000s: The rise in sushi consumption combined with the rise in celebrity culture, particularly celebrity chefs, leads to a new opportunity for sushi chefs to brand themselves to consumers. Documentaries and television shows like *Iron Chef* introduce the world to chefs such as Jiro Ono and Masaharu Morimoto. Although sushi restaurants have historically placed an emphasis on their chefs and have often been named after them, this heightened level of exposure makes establishments helmed by celebrity chefs some of the most sought-after reservations in the world.

TERMS EVERY SUSHI LOVER SHOULD KNOW

Aburi: Meaning "broiled" or "flame seared," this is a style of serving sushi in which the fish is partly raw and partly seared, either with a torch or in other ways, such as gently pressing hot coals on top of the raw fish. Typically found in Western-style restaurants, particularly in Vancouver, Canada, this preparation method creates a different texture than serving fish either raw or fully cooked and brings out natural flavors and oils of fattier fishes.

Gari: The Japanese name for thinly sliced pickled ginger that is served with a sushi meal. Naturally a pale yellow color, *gari* might be dyed pink with either food coloring or beet juice. It should be used as a palate cleanser between bites and never combined with the sushi because the flavor will overpower the rice and fish.

Itamae: Although this term translates literally to "in front of the board," in the Western world it's commonly used to denote a sushi chef. It is, however, generally reserved only for those who have trained for years as an apprentice to a master *itamae*. The *itamae* controls the recipe, consistency, and process for making a restaurant's sushi rice, arguably the most important aspect of any establishment. A diner's relationship with the *itamae* is a critical part of the overall sushi experience, especially when ordering the omakase, which is enhanced by close interaction and communication with the chef.

Izakaya: A casual Japanese pub similar to an Irish pub or tavern that's a popular place to go after work to socialize. In fact, eating at an *izakaya* is far more common today in Japan than eating at a traditional sushi bar. Known for a slower pace and a small-plates style of service, *izakayas* are becoming more popular in Europe and America. They generally offer a full range of sake (rice wine), beers, and distilled spirits. In Japan, they also have traditional floor seating on *tatami* mats or at *horigotatsu*, a low-lying table with an open space below that allows diners to sit as if in chairs. Red paper lanterns are traditionally displayed outside Japanese *izakayas*.

Maki: Literally translated as "roll," *maki* is the general term used to describe sushi that includes rice, fish, vegetables, or other ingredients rolled inside a sheet of nori and sliced into equal pieces. It is also known as *norimaki*. We explore the various kinds of maki and other types of sushi on page 25.

Makisu: A bamboo mat that sushi chefs use to form *maki* sushi.

Nori: Seaweed that is dried and flattened into sheets that can be used for making sushi, among other dishes. Nori is most commonly used in maki rolls and hand rolls. Small strips may be used in nigiri to fasten toppings like *tako* (octopus) or *kani* (crab) to the rice.

Oishii: This Japanese word means "delicious." If you love a dish your sushi chef serves, it is always a good idea to say this!

Omakase: A multicourse meal prepared especially for you by a sushi chef that is traditionally enjoyed at the sushi counter. Meaning "leave it up to you" or "to entrust," this style of service allows your chef to be creative and provide special dishes, perhaps ones not available on the restaurant's menu, at a cheaper total cost than if you ordered the same amount à la carte. Still, the omakase option can be quite expensive, so be sure to find out the cost before ordering. Omakase can consist of ten to twenty items, each served individually and usually starting with leaner fishes and progressing to fattier ones. We highly recommend the omakase experience to all sushi lovers; for more information, see page 77.

Sake: An alcoholic beverage made from the fermentation of rice, sake is the national alcoholic beverage of Japan. It is often referred to as rice wine. Like wine, sake might be served at room temperature or chilled but has a slightly higher alcohol content. Unlike wine, sake may also be served heated like tea or coffee.

Umami: A fifth category of taste after bitter, salty, sweet, and sour. Umami means "deliciousness" in Japanese, and it is generally associated with the taste of glutamates found in aged cheese, fatty meats, and sushi items such as tuna and various shellfish. Japanese chemist Kikunae Ikeda coined the term around the turn of the twentieth century. Ikeda was the first chemist to isolate the chemical monosodium glutamate (MSG), which became widely used as a flavor enhancer in Chinese food and other cuisines, as well as processed and canned items in the decades that followed.

TYPES OF SUSHI

In addition to lending itself to an array of fillings, sushi can take a variety of shapes and forms. In the styles described below, you will notice that the word *sushi* changes to *zushi* when it appears as a suffix, as in *makizushi* or *chirasizushi*. If you see the word *zushi* in your sushi dining travels, note that there is no difference in meaning. The *z* spelling indicates the change in pronunciation.

Chirashizushi: Also known as *chirashi*, this is a bowl of sushi rice topped with a variety of ingredients that can include fish, vegetables, shredded omelet, and other garnishes. In Japanese, *chirashi* means "scattered."

Gunkanmaki: A sushi roll in which a wide strip of nori is wrapped vertically around a rice ball, leaving space at the top to be filled with soft or loose ingredients like *uni* (sea urchin) or *ikura* (salmon roe). The name means "battleship roll," referring to its shiplike shape.

Inarizushi: A pouchlike piece of thin, deep-fried tofu that is seasoned with mirin (sweet Japanese cooking wine), soy sauce, dashi (fish broth), and sugar. It's often filled with sweet sushi rice or other ingredients. It is named after the Shinto god Inari, who is said to have a fondness for tofu.

Nigiri: Also known as *edo-mae*, this popular form of sushi consists of a hand-pressed cylinder of rice topped with a single piece of fish, vegetable, meat, omelet, or tofu. The name comes from the Japanese word for "grip" and refers to the way the piece is formed.

Norimaki: This is a traditional sushi roll in which rice, fish, vegetables, and other ingredients are rolled in a sheet of nori and sliced into equal pieces for serving. It is also known as *makizushi* and *maki*. The name breaks down into the Japanese words *maki*, meaning "to roll," and *nori*, referring to the seaweed wrapping. In addition to nori, *makizushi* can be rolled in soy paper or cucumber. Variations include:

- *Hosomaki* ("skinny roll"): a long, thin roll typically featuring one ingredient, like salmon or tuna

- *Futomaki* ("fat roll"): a thicker roll typically featuring several complementary ingredients and usually found in a bento box

- *Uramaki* ("inside-out roll"): an inside-out roll with the rice on the outside of the seaweed, often coated with tobiko (fish eggs) or sesame seeds

Oshizushi: Also known as *hakozushi*, this is a layer-cake approach to sushi. It's made by pressing layers of fish, vegetables, and rice into a rectangular pan. The stacked ingredients are then cut into rectangles, triangles, or squares for serving.

Sasazushi: Sushi consisting of rice and toppings wrapped in a bamboo leaf. Toppings may include wild vegetables, miso, shredded omelet, and salmon. The name is derived from the Japanese word *sasa*, meaning "bamboo leaf."

Sashimi: A traditional presentation of thickly sliced raw fish served without rice.

Temaki: A traditional hand roll consisting of rice, fish, and vegetables rolled into a cone of nori. It's simple and versatile but isn't ideal for sharing.

Temari: A simple form of sushi in which a small ball of pressed rice is topped with a thin layer of fish and other garnishes. Translated from the Japanese, it means "hand ball."

TYPES OF SUSHI FISH AND THEIR ORIGINS

Depending on where in the world you're ordering sushi, what you will find on a restaurant's menu is sure to vary. The following are types of sushi fish we have encountered often in our dining experiences.

Aji (horse mackerel or Japanese jack mackerel): This silvery skinned fish has a more delicate, sweeter flavor compared to other mackerels such as *sawara* (noted below) or *saba*, and it is far less oily. This sushi is often served raw with fresh grated scallions but may also be cured with vinegar and salt.

COMMON HARVEST LOCATION: Warm waters around the coast of Japan
PEAK SEASON: Summer
PREPARATION: Nigiri or sashimi

Amaebi (deep-water shrimp or sweet shrimp): Although these deep-water shrimp are harvested young and served fresh in fall and winter, they may be frozen and served year-round. (Interesting fact: *amaebi* are born male and transform into females later in their life cycle, which is when they are caught.) Best served as nigiri, *amaebi* is eaten raw without the head and has a surprisingly sweet taste. The heads of larger shrimp will often be served deep-fried, tempura style, separately; these have a texture similar to soft-shell crab and are delicious with a little dab of soy sauce.

COMMON HARVEST LOCATION: Deep cold waters of the northern Pacific Ocean, Atlantic Ocean
PEAK SEASON: Fall and winter
PREPARATION: Nigiri

Anago (saltwater eel or conger eel): *Anago* is leaner, more delicately flavored, and sweeter than *unagi* (see page 44). It is prepared differently as well, generally simmered in sake and soy sauce and served warm brushed with sweet *tsume* sauce, which is often called eel sauce. The white meat is very tender and will melt in your mouth. Though *anago* is traditionally considered the eel most appropriate for serving as sushi, it is not nearly as popular as *unagi* in Japan or around the world.

COMMON HARVEST LOCATION: Northwest Pacific Ocean, coast of Japan
PEAK SEASON: Summer
PREPARATION: Nigiri, deep-fried, or boiled

Ankimo (monkfish liver): Often called the foie gras of the sea, *ankimo* has a texture and flavor distinct from almost any other sushi item you will try. It is generally poached in sake and soy sauce, then wrapped tightly and steamed. It is chilled, sliced, and served cold or at room temperature with ponzu sauce and other garnishes. Look for it as an appetizer or perhaps as *gunkanmaki*.

COMMON HARVEST LOCATION: Northwestern Atlantic Ocean

PEAK SEASON: Year-round

PREPARATION: Steamed

Awabi (abalone): *Awabi* are edible sea snails with vibrantly colorful shells. The meat comes from the foot muscle that propels the snail and thus has a firm texture. When served raw, it has a subtle flavor with a slightly crunchy texture that is best enjoyed alone. It may be served cooked, or even while it's still alive (it will squirm slightly, so be prepared!). *Ezo awabi* is the highest grade of *awabi* and carries a hefty price tag.

COMMON HARVEST LOCATION: Cold coastal waters off of New Zealand, Japan, and South Africa

PEAK SEASON: Summer and early fall

PREPARATION: Nigiri, either raw or steamed

Engawa (fluke fin or flounder): This delicacy comes from the collagen-rich muscle around the fin of the flounder. It tends to be oily and has a chewy, almost crunchy texture. It may be served raw or *aburi* style to soften it and bring out the flavor of the oil.

COMMON HARVEST LOCATION: Atlantic Ocean floor, Pacific Ocean floor

PEAK SEASON: Summer

PREPARATION: Nigiri or sashimi

Escolar (butterfish): This is among the more controversial fishes you may find at your local sushi restaurant, under the name "white tuna" or "super white tuna." It strongly resembles fatty tuna, and many people enjoy its rich taste and silky texture. In fact, it's a type of snake mackerel with an extremely high fat content that causes significant digestive issues for some people. Escolar must bear a warning label in some countries and is completely banned in others, such as Italy and, you guessed it, Japan. Order this one at your own risk.

COMMON HARVEST LOCATION: Deep tropical waters around the world

PEAK SEASON: Year-round

PREPARATION: Sashimi

Hamachi **(yellowtail or amberjack):** This fish is native to the northwest Pacific Ocean, though it is farmed in Japan for sushi consumption worldwide. It's a seasonal favorite in the colder months, when the meat has a higher fat content that imparts a bold, buttery flavor.

Hamachi is a versatile fish that can be eaten as nigiri or as sashimi, often with jalapeño or scallions.

COMMON HARVEST LOCATION: Farm-raised off the coast of Japan

PEAK SEASON: Winter

PREPARATION: Nigiri or sashimi

Hirame (olive flounder): *Hirame* is a Japanese flounder, although other fishes may be labeled by this name, such as halibut, fluke, or any flat fish that lives horizontally oriented. In Western sushi restaurants, fluke and halibut are typically labeled *hirame*. Order it, and you'll be served a white fish with a delicate flavor; the texture may vary from soft to chewy, depending on how quickly the fish is served after being caught.

COMMON HARVEST LOCATION: Coast of Japan and all oceans

PEAK SEASON: Winter

PREPARATION: Nigiri or sashimi

Hokkigai (surf clam): *Hokkigai* belongs to a species of edible saltwater clam that is harvested by dredging the sea floor. Called the northern clam in Japan because it is found only in the cold waters of northern Japan, it has a sweet flavor with a mild aroma. *Hokkigai* can be served raw but oftentimes it's blanched, which firms the meat and turns the edges red.

COMMON HARVEST LOCATION: Northern Japan and northeastern U.S. and Canada

PEAK SEASON: Winter

PREPARATION: Nigiri, boiled

Hotate (scallop): The rich flavor, delicate texture, and sweetness of a live scallop make it one of the most delectable and underrated sushi items available. This versatile shellfish may be presented and enjoyed in a variety of ways, such as simple sashimi accompanied by a lemon slice or bit of sea salt, as a spicy scallop *temaki* with roasted seaweed, or, outside Japan, as a key component in elaborate maki rolls. The most commonly consumed portion of the scallop is the flesh of the adductor muscle. The other flesh surrounding this muscle is generally chewier but very tasty.

COMMON HARVEST LOCATION: Farm-raised off the coast of Japan

PEAK SEASON: Year-round, depending on the variety

PREPARATION: Sashimi

Ika (squid): The long tentacles of this cephalopod are eaten in other cuisines (think: fried calamari), but for sushi the body is often used. The flesh is a bit stiffer compared to other fishes and has a smooth, sweet flavor.

When fresh, it appears translucent; when left to age for a day, it will turn white. *Aori ika* is often considered the best of more than a hundred *ika* varieties.

COMMON HARVEST LOCATION: Northern Atlantic Ocean

PEAK SEASON: Winter and early spring

PREPARATION: Nigiri

Ikura (salmon roe): Borrowed from the Russian word *ikra*, *ikura* means "salmon fish eggs." Most *ikura* is frozen for easy storage and transport. These translucent spheres are filled with liquid that creates a burst of rich, savory, and salty umami flavor when you bite into them. They're often served alone or with a quail egg yolk as *gunkanmaki*. In modern sushi presentations (primarily outside of Japan), *ikura* may be combined with other items such as *uni* or *toro* to add texture and richness.

COMMON HARVEST LOCATION: Off the coast of Alaska and the Pacific Northwest

PEAK SEASON: Fall

PREPARATION: *Gunkanmaki*

Iwashi (sardine): Over three hundred species of sardine exist around the world. *Maiwashi* is the most popular sardine used in sushi. It has a bold taste and is usually paired with minced ginger or shallots. *Iwashi* can be eaten raw but because it spoils very quickly, it's usually salted and marinated in rice vinegar to both preserve and sweeten it.

COMMON HARVEST LOCATION: Coast of Japan
PEAK SEASON: Late summer and early fall
PREPARATION: Nigiri

Kampachi (rudderfish or great amberjack): The firm white flesh of *kampachi* has a nice, balanced fat content and a subtle sweetness. Similar in flavor to yellowtail, to which it is related, great amberjack has less fat. The best season to enjoy *kampachi* is summer, which is, coincidentally, the worst season for yellowtail. Although these fish can grow to as much as one hundred and fifty pounds, and over six feet in length, the more popular size for sushi are much smaller and generally weigh less than ten pounds each.

COMMON HARVEST LOCATION: Warm waters around Japan, Korea, and Hawaii
PEAK SEASON: Summer
PREPARATION: Nigiri or sashimi

Kani (crab): Many species of crab exist, but the most famous and arguably most delicious is king crab. Weighing as much as 18 pounds, these crabs offer plenty of meat that is known for its sweet and juicy flavor. Hokkaido, Japan, and Alaska are famous sources of king crab, so *kani* that comes from these locations will be considerably more expensive than crabs sourced elsewhere. This fish should not be confused with imitation crab meat (or imitation crab stick), which is used in sushi around the world and is a star ingredient in California rolls. Known as *surimi* or *kanikama*, it is a combination of pollock and other white fishes that are ground, pressed, and mixed with food coloring and crab flavoring. If you are unsure which you are being served, look at the color and texture. *Kani* is light pink, and *surimi* typically has a stark red color. *Kani* will also have natural striations and ridges in the meat; *surimi* has no such irregularities.

COMMON HARVEST LOCATION: Cold deep waters off coast of Alaska and Hokkaido, Japan

PEAK SEASON: Winter but may be frozen and served year-round

PREPARATION: Nigiri

Katsuo (bonito or skipjack tuna): This deep-red-fleshed fish is a much smaller relative of the tuna. Younger bonito may be enjoyed in late spring as a lighter yet flavorful sushi item. In early fall, bonito tends to be fattier and is often prepared *aburi* style or may be smoked. Another preparation option is to quickly grill the fish and place it over ice to allow for the flesh to constrict, creating a flavorful piece of meat. It's often served with scallions, grated garlic, or grated ginger to overcome the fish's strong scent of blood.

COMMON HARVEST LOCATION: Warm waters around the coast of Japan
PEAK SEASON: Late spring and early fall
PREPARATION: Nigiri or sashimi

Kihada maguro (yellowfin or ahi tuna): Characterized by its bright-yellow fins and finlets, *ahi* tuna is extremely common and served widely in sushi restaurants around the world. It has the mildest flavor of the three primary tuna species, so although it may be eaten raw, it is often served seared or in cooked sushi dishes. If you are purchasing tuna labeled as "sushi grade" it is likely to be yellowfin, which is considered the lowest level of tuna acceptable to be served raw. Like bigeye tuna, yellowfin is a sustainable alternative to the endangered bluefin tuna. (For a closer look at tuna, see page 46.)

COMMON HARVEST LOCATION: Wild in tropical and subtropical waters worldwide, farm-raised around the world
PEAK SEASON: Year-round
PREPARATION: Nigiri or sashimi

Kumamoto oyster: Originating in Kyushu, Japan, this small oyster has a sweet finish with very little brininess. Not technically a sushi item, the Kumamoto oyster is often served on the half shell, never with rice, as an appetizer. However, some establishments will serve it sashimi style. If you're squeamish about eating oysters, the small size and mild flavor of the Kumamoto might make it the one that changes your mind.

COMMON HARVEST LOCATION: Warm waters around the coast of Japan

PEAK SEASON: Year-round

PREPARATION: Raw on the half shell

Kuro maguro (bluefin tuna): Bluefin tuna is one of the most expensive and popular fishes on the global food market. It is the largest species of tuna as well. The typical weight of a bluefin is anywhere from 500 to 1,000 pounds, and at least one has been caught that was as large as 1,600 pounds! Compared to most other tunas, the bluefin has firmer dark-red flesh and higher fat content. As a result, if you enjoy *toro*, or the fatty part of the tuna's belly, bluefin tuna is your best option for this cut. It is generally served in highly rated establishments or those known for extremely high-quality sushi. Unfortunately, due to a lack of fishing and farming regulations, bluefin tuna is an endangered species.

COMMON HARVEST LOCATION: North Atlantic Ocean, farm-raised off the coast of Japan
PEAK SEASON: Year-round
PREPARATION: Sashimi

Mebachi maguro (bigeye tuna): Not surprisingly, this species is known for its large eyes. Bigeye tuna is generally leaner than the bluefin and is well known for its high-quality lean meat (or *akami*). It has a firm consistency and a flavor that is richer and more pronounced than that of yellowfin. Bigeye tuna thrives in both tropical and subtropical waters. Though generally much smaller than the bluefin, these fish can weigh as much as four hundred pounds.

COMMON HARVEST LOCATION: Tropical and subtropical waters, farm-raised around the world
PEAK SEASON: Year-round
PREPARATION: Nigiri or sashimi

Saba (mackerel): Mackerels are shiny fish named for their scales. Because shiny fish spoil quickly, most of the mackerel served at sushi bars has been cured with salt and then washed with rice vinegar prior to serving. Saba has a complex, strong flavor that can be described as salty, sour, and sweet with a dry aftertaste and strong smell. For this reason, it's best eaten as nigiri rather than combined with other ingredients as maki or chirashi. Known for its highly active migrations, *saba* may be harvested from waters all around the world.

COMMON HARVEST LOCATION: Japan, Canada, New England

PEAK SEASON: Fall through spring

PREPARATION: Nigiri

Sake (salmon): Perhaps America's second most popular sushi item after tuna, salmon sushi was first popularized in the United States due to its well-published health benefits and high level of omega-3 fatty acids. Because of its high potential for contamination by parasites, most salmon is frozen before being served raw. *Sake toro*, the fatty belly portion of the salmon, offers a much richer flavor than other parts of the fish. Even the salmon skin, known to store many of those healthy fats, is often used in sushi rolls or appetizers.

COMMON HARVEST LOCATION: Alaska and Pacific Northwestern waters

PEAK SEASON: Year-round

PREPARATION: Nigiri or sashimi

Sawara (Spanish mackerel): A bit richer in flavor than other white flesh fishes such as *hamachi* or *hirame*, and high in omega-3s, this fish tends to be oily but is both tender and delicious. Like tuna, good *sawara* will always be served fresh, never frozen. Wild-caught Spanish mackerel is sustainably managed and harvested according to U.S. regulations.

COMMON HARVEST LOCATION: South Atlantic Ocean, Gulf of Mexico
PEAK SEASON: Winter and early spring
PREPARATION: Nigiri or sashimi

Tai (red snapper or Japanese sea bream): This beautiful pink fish with delicate white flesh is also known as *madai*. (In fact, *madai* is just one of ten different varieties of *tai* commonly farmed in Japan and New Zealand, but the names are often used interchangeably due to the fish's popularity.) *Tai* is generally served as nigiri, which showcases a rich and slightly sweet flavor, but may also be prepared *aburi* style to help bring out more of its fatty flavor.

COMMON HARVEST LOCATION: South Atlantic Ocean, Gulf of Mexico
PEAK SEASON: Winter and spring
PREPARATION: Nigiri or sashimi

Tako (octopus): *Tako* is commonly found across the world and offers the diner a very different consistency and taste from traditional fishes. The most common preparation is to massage the *tako* in a warm bath for thirty minutes to an hour before boiling it in mirin and other ingredients to soften and tenderize the meat. With its uniquely soft texture and chew, *tako* is generally served as thinly sliced sashimi paired with slices of *sudachi* lime in Japan or slices of lemon in other countries.

COMMON HARVEST LOCATION: Warm waters around the coasts of Japan and Africa

PEAK SEASON: Early summer and winter

PREPARATION: Nigiri or sashimi

Tamago (sweet egg): This often overlooked, highly underrated sushi item takes a great deal of preparation, time, and skill to perfect. Some aficionados measure a quality sushi restaurant based on its presentation of this dish, which is a delicately rolled egg omelet. Although the recipes vary from one *itamae* to another, the ingredients usually include egg, mirin, soy sauce, salt, and sugar. Fish stock, ground shrimp, and yams also may be used. When properly cooked, *tamago* will be slightly sweet and have a soufflé-like density.

PEAK SEASON: Year-round

PREPARATION: Nigiri or sashimi

Tobiko **(flying fish roe):** Flying fish eggs have a mild sweet and salty taste and a crunchy texture. They are included in a variety of rolls, including California rolls, and can also be enjoyed as a garnish on nigiri. Tobiko is naturally orange but may be dyed other colors, such as black (using squid ink) or yellow (with yuzu). When infused with wasabi brine, the tobiko takes on a green hue, and some restaurants offer this as "wasabi tobiko"; try this with a quail egg to cut the heat and add texture.

COMMON HARVEST LOCATION: Tropical waters around the world

PEAK SEASON: Year-round

PREPARATION: *Gunkanmaki* or as a topping or filling for maki rolls

Unagi **(freshwater eel):** Not to be confused with *anago*, another variety of eel, *unagi* is rich, fatty, and boldly flavored. *Unagi* is more widely available in sushi bars around the world than *anago*. To maximize its bold flavor, it is typically grilled over charcoal, then steamed to remove the excess fat, seasoned with a sweet sauce, and grilled again. This makes the flesh crisp on the outside and tender on the inside.

The wild freshwater eel is an endangered species. Most of the supply comes from farm-raised juvenile eels caught in the wild. American eel, harvested from the northwest Atlantic Ocean and inland waters in North America, is a good alternative.

COMMON HARVEST LOCATION: Farm-raised in Taiwan, China, and Japan

PEAK SEASON: Year-round

PREPARATION: Nigiri

Uni (sea urchin): This porcupine-looking creature can be quite dangerous to handle without specialized protective gloves. The gonads are edible and best enjoyed fresh from the shell. *Uni* is a vibrant orange color and has a creamy texture and an aroma reminiscent of the sea. Authentic Japanese *uni* is found primarily in Hokkaido, Japan (also known for king crab), and shipped worldwide to be served fresh. This comes at a cost, and Japanese *uni* is often one of the most expensive options on the menu.

COMMON HARVEST LOCATION: Found in most major seas and oceans around the world

PEAK SEASON: Year-round, depending on variety

PREPARATION: *Gunkanmaki*

A WORD ABOUT TUNA

Tuna is the most widely eaten sushi fish and arguably the most important because of its versatility, flavor, and global appeal. Three primary species of tuna are commonly used for sushi: bluefin, bigeye, and yellowfin (also known as *ahi*) tuna. Bluefin is the highest quality, followed by bigeye and yellowtail, respectively. A fourth species, and lowest in quality, is albacore tuna, which is used primarily for canned tuna and "fast food" sushi, or in low-priced chain restaurants in Japan.

Let's take a closer look at this beloved fish.

SCARCITY

Bluefin tuna is the most sought-after tuna in the world. Although it has been eaten by the Japanese for centuries, prior to the early 1950s it was considered a throwaway fish, caught mostly for sport and occasionally ground up to be used for pet food. All that changed as sushi chefs in Japan started to serve the fish. A 1970s marketing campaign by Japanese airlines helped the bluefin improve its reputation. Instead of having cargo planes that shipped electronics to the United States return empty, Japanese airlines started to bring back inexpensive bluefin tuna and sell it for large profits at home. By the 1980s, giant bluefin had become a delicacy and bluefin fishing increased dramatically.

As a result of this large-scale change in attitude, along with a lack of fishing-industry regulation, the bluefin population declined by more than eighty percent from 1957 to 2012. Today the bluefin is considered a critically endangered species. But the fact that one sold for a record $3.1 million in 2019 (see page 50) suggests attitudes about consuming the fish have not changed. Alternatives include bigeye or yellowfin tuna, as well as the carefully regulated California yellowtail. Some conservationists might say that the bluefin was better off when it was considered best for pet food.

GRADING

Like diamonds, the quality of tuna is determined by a set of subjective measurements. The quality is graded on a scale of 1 to 3, with plus signs used to differentiate between various sublevels of the three ratings. A grade of 1 (or in some systems a 1+++) indicates the highest quality, which means the fish has the best of the following five indicators.

1. **Initial appearance.** This is an indicator of freshness. The highest grade of tuna will be clean, with

no visible punctures or damage to the skin and with all scales intact. The fish should be firm to the touch, with an overall color that is consistent with that of the species being inspected.

2. **Size and shape.** These are used to determine the yield of the fish. Obviously, larger tunas will produce more product and hold a higher value. Top grades go to fat, round tunas with thick bellies, which provide plenty of *toro* and are generally in the greatest demand.

3. **Color of meat.** This indicator is assessed by coring the fish from the middle and comparing the sample to the color of the meat in the tail portion. Bright-red color in both the center and the tail indicates overall good health and quality. The bloodline of the fish can also be inspected; it should be a darker red than the meat, but never brown or black.

4. **Texture of meat and fat.** These can also be carefully inspected from a cored sample. It is not uncommon to see buyers at Japanese fish markets rubbing the small samples between their fingers. They are generally looking for a texture that is smooth and slightly sticky.

5. **Fat content.** This is observed in part from the cored sample and in part by inspecting the collar, inside the cut tail, or in the belly wall, which is visible when the tuna's head is removed. Fish with thicker bellies are likely to have a high fat content. The higher the fat content, the higher the grade.

When distributors or restaurateurs in Japan bid on tuna, they call on their experience and the skill of experts at the market to choose the best quality. The process of choosing a high-quality fish is painstaking. Consistency of product is a critical factor for most sushi restaurants, and they often rely heavily on tuna grading to maintain such uniformity.

THE LUCKY TUNA

The Toyosu fish market outside Tokyo, Japan (formerly the Tsukiji market), is the most popular and largest wholesale fish market in the world. Tourists routinely flock to the market to watch the seafood auctions, and tuna auctions in particular. The first giant bluefin tuna auctioned on the first open market day of the new year is known as the "lucky tuna" and is said to bring good fortune to the buyer and the people who eat it. In 2019, a record $3.1 million was paid for one tuna that weighed 612 pounds. Normally, the giant bluefin sells for $30 to $50 per pound, but this "lucky" fish sold for more than $5,000 per pound! The buyer, a restaurateur named Kiyoshi Kimura, had won the highest bid on the lucky tuna for six consecutive years. We'd say that's pretty lucky indeed!

THE PARTS OF THE BLUEFIN TUNA

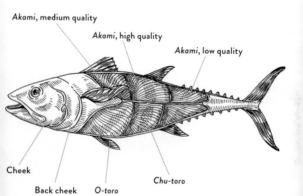

Akami, medium quality

Akami, high quality

Akami, low quality

Cheek

Back cheek   O-toro

Chu-toro

After a bluefin tuna is caught it must be immediately killed, cleaned, and frozen. Allowing the caught fish to move around too much may damage the body and cause the internal body temperature to rise. Internal heat causes the color of the meat to change from deep, bright red to brown, which is less desirable and lowers the grade of the tuna.

Two parts of the bluefin tuna are usually processed for eating: the back loin and the belly loin. That being said, the highest-caliber sushi chefs may use as much as ninety-five percent of the fish for various recipes, including ramen soup made from roasting the bones, grilled or torched portions of the skin, and broth made from the collagen-rich belly fins. Chefs who work with an entire tuna often take great pride in methodically butchering the fish and minimizing waste. The bluefin tuna butcher may use as many as five different types of knives for cutting up the fish with precision and maximizing the edible portions.

The leanest meat of the bluefin, called *akami*, is found along the back loin and the bottom of the abdomen. The highest quality *akami,* known as the *senaka*, is cut from the very center of the back loin.

Toro is the marbleized flesh found along the belly loin. Higher in fat content, it is in great demand from sushi lovers around the world and is generally the most expensive part of the fish. *Chu-toro* is the medium fatty *toro* found along the side of the belly. *O-toro* is the portion with the highest percentage of fat, found at the bottom of the belly. Today this is the costliest section of the fish, and anyone who has experienced its literal melt-in-your-mouth flavor knows it's worth every penny. However, prior to the 1950s, *toro* was considered scrap in Japan and used commonly as cat food!

At a sushi bar, you can identify the different parts of the fish based on appearance: darker meat is *akami* (lean tuna), medium-color meat is *chu-toro* (medium-fatty tuna), and the lightest color, mostly due to marbleizing, is *o-toro* (fatty tuna). An entire omakase can be prepared using only these various parts of the bluefin tuna. Consider just a few of the options that an *itamae* has:

- Sashimi and nigiri, prepared using various portions of the fish, from lean to fatty.

- *Chu-toro* steaks, served rare to medium rare in order to properly maintain the softness of the meat without sacrificing the delicious flavor that the marbleizing provides.

- Tuna tartare using lean or medium-fatty tuna. This is commonly served with a shell that can be used to scrape the meat from the ribs.

- Softer portions of skin that are grilled or deep-fried and served with ponzu sauce or other ingredients. (Note: the majority of the tuna skin is much too tough to be consumed and is generally discarded.)

THE IMPORTANCE OF SUSHI RICE

When you think of sushi, the first thing that comes to mind is usually the fish. But as any *itamae* will tell you, the key to great sushi lies in the rice. Remember that the word sushi means "vinegared rice." So, right out of the gate, there's an emphasis on this ingredient.

That emphasis isn't just in name. Generally, because the fish and vegetables are raw, the sushi chef's responsibility is to find a trusted source and make the right selections. But the rice has to be cooked, mixed, and seasoned—all of which must be done expertly by the chef.

Sushi rice is intended to enhance the flavor of the fish and other toppings. It should be served at body temperature; too cold, and the rice may harden or lose its flavor and appropriate stickiness. Properly cooked rice will be seasoned with a perfect balance of vinegar, salt, and sugar. Traditionally, sushi chefs spend years learning this craft before they even touch a piece of fish. (See page 56 for more about training to become an *itamae*.) An apprentice can spend several years just preparing the rice according to the master *itamae*'s specific recipe under the chef's strict, watchful eye. Once the master *itamae* is satisfied with the daily consistency of the rice, the apprentice will be promoted to working with other ingredients.

Over time, the chef will refine the recipe to the point that they create their own unique blend. They select the rice and the vinegar. Some will use only specific water sources or cooking methods. They spend years perfecting the balance of the mixture to produce the right taste. The rice and preparation create the possibility for differentiation from one chef to the next and can be the key factor in distinguishing good sushi from bad.

TRAINING TO BECOME AN *ITAMAE*

While the components of sushi may seem simple, an authentic Japanese sushi chef may train for up to ten years to become an *itamae*. The term *itamae* literally translates to "in front of the board," meaning that this person is responsible for everything that happens on the sushi preparation board, from making the sushi and overseeing the restaurant kitchen to entertaining guests and calculating the bill. In Japan, this is a highly revered and prestigious title.

Preparing sushi requires expert knife skills and knowledge of how to cut, clean, and prepare each fish. As described on pages 54–55, it also requires an understanding of how to properly cook the rice and apply it to a variety of dishes. Finally, it requires a culinary and creative understanding of combining ingredients to create visually stunning, perfect-tasting sushi dishes.

In Japan, students learn on the job in restaurant kitchens. Training starts with cleaning duties; a master *itamae* will monitor students' execution of washing, scrubbing, and kitchen clean-up to determine if they have the skill and motivation to complete the necessary years of training.

The first culinary task is preparing the sushi rice. Once students have consistently demonstrated an ability to make the rice perfectly without supervision, they are promoted to the level of *wakiita*, a term that translates to "closer to the chopping board." At this stage, the apprentice takes on a variety of cooking responsibilities, including preparing fish, slicing vegetables, and even making some sushi (often for take-out orders). With enough experience and time, the apprentice will be ready to use their own sushi knives (or *hocho*). When the master *itamae* gives the apprentice permission to use a *hocho* in a restaurant kitchen, it's usually an indication that the student is ready to graduate to *itamae*. The new *itamae* will have culled their craft to the point that they can work with all ingredients, wield a *hocho*, interact with guests, and manage the kitchen staff.

Sushi's growing popularity has created a demand for more chefs. Some schools now offer quicker certification courses that appeal to a younger generation, but it is still believed that intensive, on-the-job training is critical to maintaining the authentic Japanese tradition of making sushi.

NORI, SOY SAUCE, WASABI, GINGER, AND MORE

In addition to the rice and fish, a few other ingredients are important to the dining experience and overall taste of sushi. Let's explore them in more detail.

NORI

This edible seaweed is ubiquitous in maki rolls, *gunkanmaki*, hand rolls, and other Japanese dishes. It has been eaten since the sixth century and was originally consumed as a paste. The sushi world was transformed around 1750 when nori was first pressed into thin sheets using Japanese papermaking techniques, making tightly rolled combinations of fish, vegetables, and rice possible. Small strips are sometimes used in nigiri to fasten toppings like *tamago* (sweet egg) or *kani* (crab) onto the rice. Even smaller strips may be used as a topping for cooked dishes.

Roasted nori tends to be a bit crunchier and more flavorful than plain, and it can be expensive. But you can make your own: simply brush a sheet of nori with sesame oil and sprinkle with salt or other spices, then gently heat for about sixty seconds per side, until it lightens in color slightly.

SOY SAUCE

Invented in China between the third and fifth centuries, soy sauce is one of the oldest condiments in the world and is associated with all types of Asian cuisine. It was introduced to Japan in the seventh century and evolved over time. Modern Japanese soy sauce (*shoyu*) generally contains a more even ratio of soy to wheat than traditional Chinese soy sauces, making a sweeter, clearer, and thinner sauce.

Most Japanese soy sauce is brewed using a method known as *honjozo*, in which soybeans and wheat are mixed with *koji*, a kind of mold. The mixture is placed in tanks filled with brine to create an unfermented solution called *moromi*. The *moromi* ferments for six to eight months before being pressed, pasteurized, filtered, and aged or bottled. Variations on this standard method create different types of *shoyu*. The most common varieties are:

- *Koikuchi* (dark): This is the most commonly used soy sauce. It's made from an even ratio of soybeans and wheat, creating a deep color and a richer, salty taste. It's a great all-purpose soy sauce.

- *Usukuchi* (light): This type has a lighter, thinner consistency with a salty-sweet taste due to the addition of mirin. It's best for seasoning light-colored fish because it won't change the color. It can also be used as an all-purpose soy sauce in small amounts.

- **Tamari:** Similar to traditional Chinese soy sauce, tamari is made with soybeans and very little, if any, wheat. The higher soybean content imparts a strong, dense flavor, making it ideal for sushi and sashimi. Wheat-free versions are suitable for people who cannot consume gluten.

- *Genen* (reduced salt): In this more recent modification for the health-conscious sushi lover, traditional *koikuchi* sauce undergoes a special fermentation process that reduces the salt content while maintaining the flavor.

GINGER

Sweet and pickled ginger, known as *gari*, is served with sushi as a palate cleanser between bites. It is usually sliced from a young ginger root and pickled in a mixture of rice vinegar and sugar. Fine restaurants will make their own, but some will serve store-bought versions.

Although a very young ginger root may have a slightly pink hue, most are pale yellow. Vividly pink ginger likely has been dyed with food coloring or beet juice, which does not affect the flavor.

WASABI

Japanese horseradish is best served grated fresh from the wasabi plant. Technically, the wasabi we eat comes from the lower stem of the plant, although it is commonly referred to as the root. Pungent and aromatic, but not particularly spicy on its own, wasabi loses much of its flavor within about fifteen minutes of being grated. Sushi chefs will often place a small amount of wasabi between the fish and the rice in a piece of nigiri; this presentation helps to preserve the flavor a bit longer.

Very complicated to grow, Japanese horseradish is cultivated in the small, secluded mountain region of Utougi, Japan. Although it can be mass-produced, the experience of eating freshly grated Japanese wasabi is a must-try for any sushi lover. Wasabi was first used with sushi not for its pungent flavor but because it was believed to prevent foodborne illness associated with consuming raw fish. It turns out the plant contains a chemical compound called allyl isothiocyanate, which has antibacterial properties. So if you're not quite sure about that airport sushi, do yourself a favor and go heavy on the wasabi.

The pungent green paste served in most sushi restaurants around the world is probably not wasabi. The extremely high cost and limited supply of the real thing make it hard for restaurants to serve. A mix of mustard powder, horseradish, green dye, and occasionally other additives is more common. You might find this mixture in your local supermarket, sold in a tube. High-end sushi restaurants may source fresh wasabi from a highly specialized greenhouse and serve it mixed with horseradish.

ADDITIONAL COMPONENTS

You may find these additional items in your sushi meal.

Quail eggs: These are generally served as an optional topping for *gunkanmaki* such as *tobiko*, *ikura*, and *uni*, but they're delicious with lots of other foods—wagyu beef, Kumamoto oysters, and more.

Daikon radish: This white root vegetable is mildly flavored and versatile. It may be shredded and used to garnish a plate of sashimi; pickled, sliced, and rolled into thin *oshinkomaki*; served in salads; or grated for use in maki with other ingredients.

Shiso leaf: This Japanese herb is a relative of mint. It may dress up a sushi plate as a garnish or be used as an ingredient in vegetarian maki or hand rolls. It is often paired with *umeboshi*, or pickled plums.

Sauces: An *itamae* may gently brush nigiri with various sauces, such as soy sauce, citrusy ponzu, sweet-savory *tsume* (aka eel sauce), or yuzu-flavored miso sauces. The choice is generally based on what the chef thinks will bring out the natural flavors of the fish. Most sauces served with sushi will include some combination of mirin (sweet cooking wine), soy sauce, or sake, perhaps with other ingredients such as sugar and yuzu. Of course, there is also the famous "spicy mayo," which has surged in popularity around the world as a topping and dipping sauce. It is often combined with chopped fish such as tuna, scallop, yellowtail, and others in maki.

HOW TO USE CHOPSTICKS

Although there are situations, such as an omakase meal, when it is completely acceptable to eat sushi using your fingers, the true sushi lover will want to know how to use chopsticks. Like many skills, this is best learned in childhood but can be acquired later in life. Follow these simple steps to become a quick master. We can't promise you will be able to catch a fly *Karate Kid* style, but we can promise that you will proudly enjoy that first spicy tuna roll without a mess.

1. Remove the chopsticks from the package. If they are the kind of wooden chopsticks that are attached at the top, gently pull them apart. You may see a small splinter or two, but you should avoid the temptation to rub the sticks together because the chef may find this insulting. Discreetly remove the splinter with your fingers or ask for another pair. (For more on etiquette, see pages 70–76.)

2. Hold your dominant hand out in front of you as if you were going to arm wrestle someone. Place

one chopstick perpendicularly in the web of that hand with about an inch of the wide end sticking out behind your hand. Rest the middle of the chopstick on the side of your ring finger just above the fingernail. Apply slight pressure with the base of your thumb to stabilize the chopstick.

TIP: Keep your thumb straight, with only its base securing the chopstick. If you bend your thumb, you will find it much easier to lose your grip on the bottom stick.

3. Take the second chopstick and hold it gently with the face of your thumb and between your index and middle fingers. Be sure the narrow ends of

the sticks are lined up. Keep your hand relaxed, and apply gentle pressure only at the base of your thumb to hold the bottom stick in place.

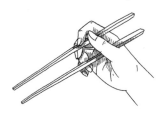

4. Allow your index and middle finger to do the work of moving the top chopstick while keeping your thumb relatively straight and still. Place the two ends of the chopsticks around a piece of sushi, pinch them closed, and pick it up.

Practice makes perfect, so the more you use chopsticks, the better you will get. Have patience and don't get too frustrated. Given that they have been in use for around 9,000 years, you won't be the first or the last person to mess this up a few times.

Although they are called chopsticks, you should neither "chop" nor "stick" with them. They are intended to pick up food, so make sure that's all you do with them. Finally, avoid picking up large pieces when you're new to this skill, and give yourself a chance to learn. Most sushi is meant to be eaten in one bite, so get that piece from your plate into your mouth and enjoy!

AT
THE
SUSHI
BAR

SUSHI ETIQUETTE

From the moment you enter a sushi restaurant until the bittersweet final bite, there is much more to know and enjoy about the meal than just the food. This dining experience can vary greatly between restaurants, cities, and countries around the world. The etiquette required at a renowned restaurant such as Sukiyabashi Jiro in Japan be dramatically different from what is expected at a sushi spot in your local strip mall. That said, knowing the basic expectations will prepare you for whatever lies ahead and, at the very minimum, will impress whoever you're with.

WELCOME: *IRASSHAIMASE!*

Ever walked into a sushi restaurant and felt overwhelmed when four chefs seemed to announce your arrival in Japanese? Most likely they were offering the traditional greeting of *irasshaimase* (pronounced "ee-RA-shy-MAS-say"), meaning "welcome" or "come in." This has long been a common way for many Japanese business owners to greet customers as a sign of respect and to show that they are ready to serve you. A simple smile or nod of acknowledgment will suffice, but the more adventurous diner will reply *ojama shimasu* ("oh-JAH-mah she-MAH-soo"), which literally translates to "sorry to interrupt your work" but is a way to show your humble appreciation for the warm welcome. *Yoroshiku* ("yo-ROHSH-koo"), meaning "please be good to me," or even *konnichiwa* ("koh-NEE-chee-wah"), meaning "hello," might surprise the chef and wow your dining companions.

Upon entering the establishment, you will be offered a choice of sitting either at the sushi bar or at a traditional dining table. If you are in a large group you may consider table seating, but a true sushi lover will sit at the bar to enjoy the dining experience and interaction with the sushi chef. (Most of the following tips pertain to the sushi bar.)

When you first sit at the sushi bar, you might glimpse different fishes through glass. These large pieces of fish are called *saku* blocks, and they will be sliced into smaller pieces after you order. Ask the chef about special items that may be available, but never inquire what is "fresh." All sushi restaurants should be serving fish that is properly prepared. If the chef does respond to such a question, the answer might imply that other items are somehow below standard; at worst, the question may offend the chef.

CHOPSTICKS

Using chopsticks is always an option when eating sushi, but using your hands is also considered acceptable; it's even encouraged when enjoying an omakase, where each piece of sushi is served one at a time. However, eating sashimi with your hands is not appropriate, so you will inevitably need chopsticks at some point in your meal. Avoid rubbing wooden chopsticks together after separating them. Because doing so is necessary only with low-quality chopsticks, this is considered offensive to the chef and the establishment. If you spot a splinter on one of your chopsticks, you may request a new pair from the waitstaff.

ONE BITE

With the exceptions of *temaki* and *inari*, sushi should be eaten in a single bite. Attempting to eat a piece in multiple bites will result in a mess on your plate and a stern glare from a sushi chef. After all, the chef has likely worked for years to perfect the consistency of rice and the precise cut of the fish and has delicately molded the piece together to the perfect blend of flavors while adding just the right amount of wasabi to finalize the perfect piece of sushi just for you to enjoy . . . So yeah, one bite.

Sushi serving sizes in the early 1900s were significantly larger than the current bite size that we are familiar with today. Following World War II, American-occupied Japan suffered a rice shortage, and the U.S. military responded by rationing what rice was available. They even went so far as to attempt to close sushi restaurants across the country! Ultimately this did not come to pass, but rules placed on restaurants required that they use only the rationed portion of rice from patrons who brought their own. The result, of course, was smaller portions, which is a custom we continue today. (Fortunately, we don't need to bring our own rice.)

SOY SAUCE AND WASABI

One of the most common mistakes that sushi patrons make relates to soy sauce. We mix large amounts of wasabi into the stuff, then dunk the sushi into the mixture and create a soupy mess that drips onto our plate. Soy sauce and wasabi should enhance, not detract from, the distinctive taste of each fish and the carefully prepared rice.

Throughout Japan and in authentic sushi restaurants

around the world, chefs often add a small amount of wasabi between the rice and the fish in nigiri (depending on the fish). Although you may not know if your chef has done this, please avoid the temptation to look under the fish by picking it up with your chopsticks or your finger. This destroys the integrity of the nigiri and will likely insult the *itamae*.

While it is acceptable to add a small amount of wasabi to your soy sauce, less is more. Too much wasabi will overpower the flavor of the fish. To use soy sauce with nigiri, turn the sushi on its side and pick up the fish and rice together, using chopsticks or your fingers. Lightly dip the fish side only into the soy sauce, then place it in your mouth. It is important not to dip the rice into the sauce for two reasons: It drowns out the flavor of the rice, and it causes the rice to fall apart and risks the integrity of the sushi that your chef has worked so hard to prepare.

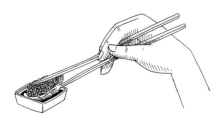

For sashimi, use your chopsticks to place a bit of wasabi directly on the fish. Then fold the fish, which makes it easier to hold, and if you want, dip it lightly into the soy sauce before eating. Letting the fish sit in the soy sauce or submerging it is a quick way to ruin the taste and frustrate a chef.

Occasionally your *itamae* will brush the top of the fish either with soy sauce or *tsume* sauce. This is most commonly done at the sushi bar or during an omakase. This addition creates a more beautiful presentation but also flavors the fish in the amount your chef deems necessary to enhance it. If you are served a piece in this manner, do not dip it in more soy sauce; simply enjoy as the chef has prepared it.

> **TIP:** When eating *gunkanmaki* made with *uni*, *ikura*, or any loose filling that cannot be turned over and dipped into soy sauce, dip a piece of ginger into the soy sauce and then gently paint the top of your filling with it and eat it.

GINGER

Ginger is not to be combined with sushi under any circumstance. It will completely overpower the nuanced flavors in the rice and the fish. Eat as much as you like between bites to prepare your mouth for the next piece; the chef or waitstaff will likely notice if you run low and replenish as needed.

GRATUITY

Generally speaking, gratuity should follow the customs of where your restaurant is located. In Japan, gratuity is generally included in the bill. In Europe, a five to ten percent gratuity is considered acceptable. In America, a tip of fifteen to twenty percent is generally expected. If there is a jar for tips on the sushi bar and you enjoy your meal, we suggest adding a little something extra for the chef on your way out, particularly if you don't have the chance to sit at the sushi bar.

THE OMAKASE EXPERIENCE

Omakase is a Japanese term meaning "to entrust" or "I leave it up to you." The omakase at a sushi bar is similar to a tasting menu; by ordering this meal you invite the sushi chef to surprise you with several courses of sashimi, nigiri, maki, and various other items, such as soup or hot cooked dishes. Often the omakase offers the *itamae* a chance to showcase items that are in season or something not offered on the restaurant's regular menu. In America, the experience may include a greater variety of offerings, whereas in Japan omakase tends to focus exclusively on traditional sushi.

The omakase is an exciting opportunity for the sushi connoisseur to enjoy a personalized experience and perhaps try something new. Although this style of meal varies from one restaurant and chef (and diner) to another, there are some basic components you can expect during an omakase and some basic "rules" to consider.

The majority of the meal will be sushi items, possibly following an appetizer. The *itamae* will likely brush a small amount of soy sauce or *tsume* sauce on the fish prior to serving. Dipping the piece in soy sauce is discouraged; you can trust that the chef has used the appropriate amount. Lighter, mild-flavored fishes such as yellowtail (*hamachi*) or flounder (*hirame*) will be served early on. As the meal progresses you can expect heavier, fattier fishes such as fatty tuna (*o-toro*) or sea urchin (*uni*). Throughout the omakase, your taste buds evolve, allowing you to taste more of the fat in the heavier fishes. By serving in this order, the *itamae* gives you the best opportunity to detect the specific flavors of every item.

Take a moment to enjoy the visual attributes of each course, but don't let it sit too long. The sushi is meant to be enjoyed immediately after it is served, and often your chef will watch your expression to see if you are happy or not. It is always good form to be honest with your chef, because your feedback about a particular fish will allow him to tailor the remainder of the meal to your taste.

TIP: Buy the chef a drink, or if you're BYO'ing, share a glass of the wine, beer, or sake you brought. This gesture is recommended any-time you're eating a meal at the sushi bar, but it's especially thoughtful when partaking in an omakase experience.

The omakase will consist of ten to twenty pieces, depending on the chef, the dishes served, and the price. Toward the end of the meal you might expect a hand roll, a small maki roll, or a course featuring sweet egg (*tamago*). Dessert is not commonly served with omakase. Typically the chef will indicate that the meal is nearing its end. When the omakase is complete, you are welcome to order items from the restaurant menu. Or if you enjoyed something during the meal, feel free to order more of it; this will likely please the chef. Soup or a cup of hot green tea after the meal can aid digestion.

Other tips for making the most of the omakase:

- **No menu.** Don't be surprised if you don't see a written menu; there's a good chance the chef will decide what to serve as the meal unfolds, responding to your preferences and reactions to dishes as they are served. For this reason, we recommend that you enjoy omakase at the sushi bar, so that you and the chef can discuss the meal. Picky eaters and people with food allergies may not appreciate the omakase for this reason; if you take the plunge, be sure to inform your chef in advance of specific dislikes or restrictions.

- **Quality counts.** Order the omakase at restaurants where the ingredients are fresh and the chef or restaurant is known for quality sushi. Avoid this style of eating at larger chain restaurants or restaurants offering a limited variety of fish.

- **The expense.** Omakase typically comes with a substantial price tag. We've seen it offered at prices ranging from $50 to $150, but depending on location it can cost much, much more. The omakase at the high-end restaurant Masa in New York City, for example, *starts* at $595 per person. If price is a concern, it is perfectly acceptable to ask the chef or waitstaff for the omakase cost as well as available options, such as skipping the sake pairing or the pricey wagyu beef course. Some restaurants offer a more affordable lunch omakase.

The omakase at Sukiyabashi Jiro in Tokyo costs 30,000 yen per seating (approximately $300). This would be an expensive meal at any upscale, white-tablecloth restaurant. But consider that Sukiyabashi seats only nine people at the bar, there is no restroom, and your meal can be completed in as little as twenty minutes. That amounts to $15 per bite! However, the tiny restaurant enjoys a rare three-star Michelin rating, which speaks to how delicious the sushi is. Still, this rushed experience is not for everyone and offers little opportunity for diners to interact with the chef.

- **Damp towel to begin (and possibly end) your meal.** This will be provided for you to clean your hands. If you intend to eat sushi with your hands (this is perfectly acceptable), use it sparingly at first so that you can reuse it throughout the meal.

- **Japanese green tea.** This is also commonly served with the omakase free of charge, but if it is not complimentary, we highly recommend ordering it as an accompaniment and palate cleanser.

- **Communication.** We strongly encourage the omakase diner to communicate with the chef, to ask questions, and not to be timid during the meal. Inquiring how something should be eaten, where a particular fish is from, or what items are similar to something you enjoyed will lead to a better experience and continue to enhance your love for sushi. If there is a language barrier between you and your chef, try indicating non-verbally, such as by smiling, when you find something particularly delicious.

POPULAR À LA CARTE ITEMS

Around the world, sushi has evolved to reflect local culture and cuisine. In countries where foods are heavily spiced, you'll find sushi served with hot sauces and peppers, whereas other populations may favor fresh-caught fish and local ingredients. What is popular may vary through your travels, but the following items are commonly found at sushi restaurants outside of Japan.

ROLLS

California roll: This ubiquitous maki roll (which is believed to hail from Canada; see page 19) is not usually made with raw fish. The seafood inside is imitation crabmeat, also known as *surimi*, which is formed from minced fish, typically pollock. Avocado and cucumber are also rolled into this *uramaki*, or inside-out roll.

Dragon roll: Another maki roll with the rice on the outside, this is filled with crunchy shrimp that is battered and fried (known as tempura) and cucumber. It is topped with thinly sliced avocado and may be finished with a spicy sauce or *tobiko*.

Philadelphia roll: The main ingredients of a Philadelphia roll are salmon, either raw or smoked, plus cucumber and cream cheese. Madame Saito, a Tokyo-trained sushi chef who has worked in Philadelphia for decades and is the self-proclaimed "queen of sushi," claims to have introduced this roll at a sushi-making event in the 1980s after being inspired by bagels and lox. When she unveiled her creation, she says, the crowd came up with the name.

Rainbow roll: This roll incorporates several different fishes and displays their bold colors outside the rice, hence its name. A traditional California roll is wrapped with layers of salmon, tuna, sea bass or other white fish, and thinly sliced avocado.

Spicy scallop hand roll: This *temaki* is a wonderful blend of flavors and textures. The crunchy, salty, roasted seaweed outside combines perfectly with the sweetness and delicate softness of the raw scallop and the subtle bite from the spicy mayonnaise.

Spicy tuna roll: This roll is many diners' introduction to raw fish. Minced tuna is mixed with a spicy mayo and wrapped into a maki roll, either inside or outside the rice and nori.

Spider roll: The defining ingredient here is tempura-fried soft-shell crab. Other fillings can include cucumber, lettuce, and avocado, and the roll is typically drizzled with *tsume* sauce. Spider rolls usually feature only cooked ingredients, making this a good option for sushi newcomers or anyone who can't eat raw fish.

Tiger roll: This is another roll filled with tempura-fried ingredients that's popular because it doesn't include raw fish. (That, and fried food is delicious.) It generally includes shrimp tempura inside, with avocado and shrimp on the outside.

NIGIRI AND SASHIMI

Eel: If you're introducing eel to a budding sushi lover, we recommend calling it by its Japanese name, *unagi*, first and then explaining what it is after they have tried it (and loved it). In our experience this fish can be intimidating for first-timers. That said, it is one of the most popular cooked sushi items on menus around the world—so much that in 2013 the Japanese government declared wild *unagi* an endangered species. Much of what you're likely to be served in a restaurant is farm-raised eel.

Salmon, yellowtail, and tuna: You're likely to find these three fishes on most sushi restaurant menus, especially outside Japan. Among the more popular sushi fish, they are often served together as lunch specials because of their popularity and relatively low cost.

Shrimp: This is a popular and appealing option for sushi newbies because it is served fully cooked and is an ingredient that many folks have eaten before. If you want to introduce tentative eaters, especially children, to sushi, shrimp rolls or nigiri are recommended. Sushi connoisseurs may seek out *amaebi*, a sweet shrimp that is served raw and has a soft texture.

OTHER DISHES

Yellowtail with jalapeño: First developed by famed sushi chef Nobuyuki "Nobu" Matsuhisa, this dish has become wildly popular around the world. Thin slices of yellowtail are topped with sliced jalapeño and drizzled with ponzu sauce. The combination of the tangy citrus sauce, the rich flavor of the fish, and the crunch and heat of the jalapeño make this a delicious alternative to yellowtail sashimi.

Tuna tartare: This dish of chopped raw tuna tossed with seasonings such as sesame ginger sauce or avocado is popular as an introduction to raw fish. Look for it as an appetizer, often served with crispy wonton chips.

THE WORLD'S MOST EXPENSIVE SUSHI ROLL

Traditional Japanese sushi tends to be minimalist, but chefs in other countries have created complex, unique sushi by adding unexpected sauces, fillings, and toppings. Perhaps no better example exists than the roll created in 2010 by the so-called karat chef, Angelito Araneta Jr., which earned the Guinness World Record for most expensive sushi. The five-piece maki roll is filled with premium Norwegian salmon and foie gras, wrapped in 24-karat gold leaf instead of seaweed, and garnished with three Mikimoto pearls and a .25 carat diamond. Amazingly, every part of this roll is edible, and it sells at Araneta's restaurant in Manila, the Philippines, for the equivalent of $1,978 USD.

EXPANDING YOUR PALATE

The world of sushi is vast. If you've been enjoying this cuisine for several years you may be ready to take your passion to the next level, or you may just be bored ordering the same tried-and-true menu items. For starters, ask the chef at your favorite sushi restaurant for recommendations; based on your preferred fishes, the chef may be able to offer you items with similar textures or fattiness. Inquire about current specials (but avoid asking "what's fresh"; this may insult the chef). Or order the omakase, which is an exciting, interactive way to taste a variety of fishes and other offerings not on the restaurant's menu; asking questions during this meal will help you learn the kinds of fish you enjoy so you can seek them out in the future. (See page 77 for more about omakase.)

Expanding your sushi palate depends, of course, on what you've already eaten. The following items are a bit harder to find and worth seeking out.

AKAMUTSU (ROSY SEA BASS)

This fish has extremely large eyes and a black throat; it's also known as *nodoguro* or black throat sea perch. Its tender white flesh is similar to *kinmedai* (see page 90), but a bit oilier and with higher fat content. The flavor is slightly sweet. *Akamatsu* is often served *aburi* style (torched) to bring out the flavor of the fat.

COMMON HARVEST LOCATION: Deep seas off Japan's coast
PEAK SEASON: Fall and winter
PREPARATION: Nigiri or sashimi

KANPYO (CALABASH GOURD)

The calabash gourd, sometimes called bottle gourd, is a large vegetable that grows to an average weight of about 12 pounds. Wide strips of the flesh, cut to the size of nori paper, are left to bake in the sun or dehydrated for two days. It may be served simmered on its own, rolled into a thin maki roll called *kanpyo-maki*, or combined with other fillings into a larger *futomaki* roll. *Kanpyo-maki* is well known as the first traditional roll of what is now Tokyo, Japan.

COMMON HARVEST LOCATION: Tochigi, Japan
PEAK SEASON: Late July through September
PREPARATION: *Kanpyo-maki*

KINMEDAI (SPLENDID ALFONSINO OR GOLDEN EYE SNAPPER)

Known for its large eyes and bright-red skin, *kinmedai* is found in deep waters, commonly off the southern coast of Japan. It is often served with some of the skin left on and cooked *aburi* style to help release umami flavors from the high oil and fat content. It may also be quickly boiled and then placed in ice to tenderize it.

COMMON HARVEST LOCATION: Deep southern Japanese waters

PEAK SEASON: Winter and early spring

PREPARATION: Nigiri or sashimi

NATTO (FERMENTED SOYBEANS)

Natto is a popular dish in Japan that may be homemade or sold refrigerated in markets. Many people enjoy it for breakfast. Small soybeans are washed, soaked, and steamed before being combined with a bacterial culture and fermented for up to one day. Rich in potassium and vitamin B12, the dish has a sticky, sometimes stringy texture, bold flavor, and pungent aroma. It can be enjoyed on its own or served as a hand roll, although *natto* hand rolls tend to be cylindrical rather than cone shaped.

PREPARATION: *Temaki*

SHIRAKO (MILT OR COD SPERM)

For some sushi lovers, trying *shirako* is the ultimate in adventurous eating. This is the Japanese name for cod sperm sacs, although it may be used to refer to sperm harvested from anglerfish, salmon, puffer fish, or squid. *Shirako* translates literally to "white children." The sacs have the appearance of a cluster of white beans or a scoop of macaroni salad, with a salty flavor and a soft, creamy texture. *Shirako* is believed to be good for the skin and contains high levels of vitamins B12 and D. It may be prepared in a number of ways including tempura style, crispy on the outside with a creamy center, or served raw in *gunkanmaki* with ponzu sauce and topped with grated daikon or green onion. *Shirako* tends to be expensive and is a common item in Japanese *izakayas* (pubs) but may be harder to come by elsewhere.

COMMON HARVEST LOCATION: Cold waters of the Sea of Japan

PEAK SEASON: Winter

PREPARATION: *Gunkanmaki*

TORIGAI (JAPANESE COCKLE)

Also known as the bird clam, this shellfish has an intensely colored purple-and-white flesh that is typically blanched to further brighten the hue, though it can be eaten raw. Available only briefly in spring, it has a soft, chewy texture with a sweet flavor and distinct aroma.

COMMON HARVEST LOCATION: East China and Yellow Seas

PEAK SEASON: April/May

PREPARATION: Nigiri

A NOTE ABOUT *FUGU* (PUFFER FISH OR BLOWFISH)

Authentic wild *fugu* is a delicacy served as thinly sliced sashimi that has you quite literally taking your own life in your hands when you eat it. The internal organs of this fish contain a poison known as tetrodotoxin, which is one hundred times more potent than cyanide and has no known antidote. If the fish is not properly prepared, the poison may contaminate the meat and put the eater at risk of death.

Needless to say, you are not likely to find this dish at your local sushi bar; chefs in Japan are required to undergo extensive training and be certified to serve it. Most of the chefs who take the rigorous certification test fail. Restaurateurs in Japan must be fully licensed to sell and prepare *fugu*, and the delicacy sells for as much as $200 USD per dish. Thanks to these high safety standards, only about three *fugu*-related deaths a year are reported, likely caused by inexperienced and recreational cooking. Regardless, the fish has been banned in the European Union and is not a popular request at restaurants around the world, despite that a nontoxic farm-raised option is available. Perhaps another reason for the fish's unpopularity: the taste is said to be quite bland.

The potential risk of eating this notorious fish was hilariously featured in a 1991 episode of *The Simpsons* entitled "One Fish, Two Fish, Blowfish, Blue Fish," in which Homer eats *fugu* sushi that has been prepared by an inexperienced chef. Afterward, alone in the doctor's office, he murmurs to himself, "Try something new, Homer . . . What will it hurt you, Homer . . . I never heard of a poison pork chop!"

HOW TO PAIR SAKE, BEER, AND WINE WITH SUSHI

Japanese green tea may be the most common, and often a free, accompaniment for sushi, but sushi lovers may enjoy something stronger with their meal. Sake, the national alcoholic beverage of Japan and a standard partner for sushi since the 1930s, is a natural fit, and beer and wine can also enhance the dining experience. Read on for tips to make the most of these pairings.

SAKE

Sake is an alcoholic beverage made from fermented rice. It is often referred to as rice wine. To make it, grains of rice are scrubbed of their outer layers in a process known as polishing, leaving the starchy center. This inner portion of the rice is full of the starch that is essential to the fermentation process and provides better aroma and flavor. Sake typically has a slightly higher alcohol content than wine, between 18 percent and 20 percent. It may be served at room temperature, chilled, or heated, like tea or coffee. Although the temperature that a sake is served at depends on the variety, the season, and personal preference, typically better-quality sake is served only at room temperature or chilled so that the nuances of fragrance and taste are not lost.

Similar to wine, the variety of sake is vast and can be intimidating for first-time consumers. Factors such as aging, pasteurization, filtering, and polishing can all influence the final product. For more detailed information we recommend the 2014 book *Sake Confidential* by John Gauntner.

> **TIP:** In Japan, the term *sake* refers to alcoholic drinks in general, including wine and beer. So although you might be safe ordering a sake at an *izakaya* in Barcelona, Spain, this request might confuse a bartender in Japan. In an authentic Japanese *izakaya* or similar establishment, you will want to request *nihonshu*, meaning "Japanese alcohol."

There are four main categories of quality sake, based on the degree of polishing: *honjozo-shu*, *junmai-shu*, *ginjo-shu* (or *junmai ginjo-shu*), and *daiginjo-shu* (or *junmai daiginjo-shu*). In broad terms, the more the grains are polished, the higher the quality of sake, and the higher the price of the bottle.

- *Junmai-shu,* which is Japanese for "pure rice sake," consists of water, yeast, *koji* (a type of mold that breaks down the rice), and rice that has been polished to at least 70 percent of its original size. This is a good option for the first-time sake drinker. It pairs well with fatty and heavy sushi such as salmon roe, fatty tuna, monkfish liver, and yellowtail, as well as most American-style maki rolls. But it can overpower lighter fishes.

- *Honjozo-shu,* meaning "genuine brew sake," is similar to *junmai-shu* but has a small amount of distilled alcohol added to soften the flavor and aroma. Of the four types listed here, it is generally considered the least desirable; however, for some, its smooth flavor and fragrance are just the right fit.

- *Junmai ginjo-shu,* which means "pure rice, special brew sake," is polished to at least 60 percent. Considered a superior grade, it is highly recommended for experienced sake drinkers who want to explore premium brands. It typically costs more than *junmai-shu.* Try pairing it with the lighter early courses of an omakase dinner.

- *Junmai daiginjo-shu,* or "pure rice, very special brew sake," is polished to at least 50 percent and is the most premium grade. Like *ginjo-shu,* this sake pairs well with lean fishes such as halibut, sweet shrimp, or abalone.

Futsu-shu, or "table sake," is a grade lower than the ones mentioned above. It is often polished to 20 percent to 25 percent, and its low price makes it a perfect choice for cooking.

> **TIP:** Never pour your own sake! Pouring sake for others in your group is a means for creating interactions and acknowledging the needs of others before yourself. It is a wonderful custom to follow. Nevertheless, don't be the sake police and call people out who are not familiar with the practice. Your friends won't want to share sake (or anything else) with you in the future, and then you will be forced to pour your own sake because you will be drinking alone.

Like wine, different sakes can be sweeter or drier depending on the amount of residual sugar, alcohol, and water they contain. Lucky for us, bottles bear a number known as the sake meter value (abbreviated SMV) that represents this quality. Ratings range from very sweet at -15 to very dry at +15. A number on the label that's preceded by a plus or minus is the sake's

SMV; a rating of 0 indicates a neutral variety. Keep in mind that the taste may vary based on the alcohol content and the temperature at which the sake is served.

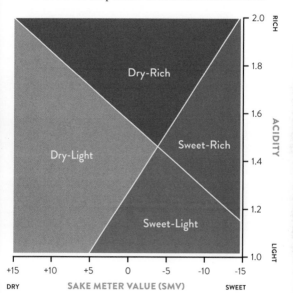

BEER AND WINE

When it comes to beer and wine, it can be difficult to find a single choice that will pair well with an entire sushi dinner, let alone a full omakase. Instead, we recommend choosing a beverage that can complement the sushi experience and leave the fish as the main attraction. Light Japanese lagers such as Kirin, Sapporo, or Asahi all work perfectly. Lighter pilsners such as Saint Arnold Summer Pils or Terrapin Sound Czech Pils pair nicely, but some pilsners may be too bitter and distract from the sushi. Witbiers and hefeweizens generally are good choices as well. Avoid dark beers like stouts or porters and hoppier brews like IPAs.

Wines with low tannins, a delicate flavor, and lower acidity partner well with lean fish. Fattier fishes can stand up to slightly bolder wines with higher acidity. Because most meals will consist of a combination of both types of fish, we recommend sticking with white wine or light reds. Crisp chablis, rosé, chardonnay, and dry riesling are all good choices. A dry champagne will work with most anything. If you prefer red wine, try a pinot noir from the Willamette Valley or a similarly light-bodied gamay from New Zealand. A light merlot may work, but avoid anything that will overpower the flavor and fragrance of the fish.

FAMOUS SUSHI CHEFS AROUND THE WORLD

Enjoying sushi around the globe is a wonderful way to broaden your knowledge and deepen your love for this cuisine. Trying sushi in a new place can expose you to local variations, traditional offerings, and fresh high-quality ingredients not available where you live. Following are five famous sushi chefs worth seeking out if you have the opportunity in your travels.

JIRO ONO
Sukiyabashi Jiro, Ginza, Japan

Born in 1925, Itamae Jiro Ono is widely regarded as the greatest living sushi chef. At over 90 years of age, he continues to work daily and oversees a strict level of quality at his restaurant, Sukiyabashi Jiro, which he opened in 1965. Though renowned in Japan for decades, he became more widely known after a documentary about him and his restaurant, called *Jiro Dreams of Sushi*, was released in 2011.

Sukiyabashi Jiro has earned the rare accolade of three Michelin stars, joining a select few other restaurants such as Azurmendi in Spain, Robuchon au Dôme in Macau, and Alinea in Chicago. What sets Jiro's restaurant apart from all of them is the limited seating (just nine guests), the fast pace of your meal (it will be over within an hour of your arrival), and the fact that you'll have to walk next door to use a restroom.

Reservations are extremely difficult to get, especially for tourists; the restaurant is fully booked months in advance and has an extensive waiting list. Former U.S. president Barack Obama was able to snag a seat for dinner in 2014, but it didn't hurt that he was dining with the Japanese prime minister Shinzo Abe. Jiro's son Yoshikazu Ono is an incredible chef in his own right and in 2003 opened a second restaurant called Sukiyabashi Jiro Roppongi Hills. This location boasts an impressive two Michelin stars, is generally less expensive than the original, and is far easier to get into.

MASAYOSHI "MASA" TAKAYAMA
Masa, New York, New York

Growing up in a small rural town a few hours north of Tokyo, Masa helped his parents and siblings working in a fish shop and catering business, cutting fish and delivering it on his bicycle. He worked for eight years as an apprentice in Ginza—a district of Tokyo renowned as having the greatest sushi restaurants and chefs in the world—before moving to California at the age of twenty-four. He opened his first restaurant a few years later and another, called Ginza Sushiko, in 1987, sourcing top-quality ingredients such as fish flown directly from the famous Tsukiji fish market in Tokyo. He soon earned a reputation with local celebrities and other wealthy diners for offering unique creations with a hefty price tag. In 2004 he opened his restaurant Masa in New York City, which serves one of the most expensive sushi dinners in the world. Masa's omakase, which starts at $595 per person, includes his signature dish, black-caviar-topped *toro*, plus other decadent offerings such as *uni* with black truffle and *fugu* with edible gold flakes. In 2009 the restaurant became the first Japanese restaurant in the United States to earn three Michelin stars, and it has maintained the honor for nearly ten years.

MASAAKI KOYAMA
Masaaki's Sushi, Geeveston, Australia

Masaaki Koyama grew up in a small rural village in Japan called Wakayama, where he was introduced to making sushi by his grandmother and father. He left home at age eighteen to pursue his dream of becoming a sushi chef in Osaka. He worked hard on his craft for several years before he met his wife, Lucy, who was traveling in Japan from her hometown in the Huon region of Tasmania. They married and eventually he followed her to this small logging town, called Geeveston, known primarily for forestry and apple orchards. Soon after, he decided to open a restaurant to bring a taste of Japan to the people of Geeveston. In fact, many of his early customers had never heard of sushi and initially were not thrilled with the idea of eating raw fish.

Today his restaurant, Masaaki's Sushi, is open only two days a week and the sushi sells out regularly. He sources fish and fresh produce locally, including vegetables and spices grown in his home garden. Diners are known to have traveled from around the world to this small town, largely to enjoy his sushi. Unlike the über-traditional style of some renowned sushi chefs like Jiro Ono, Masaaki creates a laid-back environment and likes to chat with his customers.

KAKINUMA YOSHIHARU
Sushi Shikon, Sheung Wan, Hong Kong

Kakinuma Yoshiharu practically has the art of sushi making in his blood; both his father and grandfather were sushi chefs. He grew up playing and working at the family restaurant and going to the fish market with his grandfather, with whom Kakinuma was very close. His grandfather taught him about discipline and the importance of quality ingredients. His father felt it was best for Kakinuma to learn outside the family to create his own success. He was introduced to master chef Masahiro Yoshitake and served as an apprentice chef under him. Yoshitake took great interest in Kakinuma's abilities and trained him personally, which is highly unusual; typically an apprentice chef will be trained by assistant chefs for years before beginning hands-on learning from a master chef. After this training Kakinuma moved to the United States and for the next decade continued to hone his craft in Atlanta and New York. In 2012 Yoshitake invited his former apprentice to serve as the executive chef at his new restaurant, Sushi Shikon, in Hong Kong. During Kakinuma's tenure the restaurant became the first Hong Kong restaurant to be awarded three Michelin stars. Like Masaaki, Kakinuma interacts more with patrons than traditional sushi chefs, a trait he picked up in his ten years in the U.S., and he credits the restaurant's success to good communication with fishermen and his endless passion for improving his skills. His signature dish is steamed abalone cooked in abalone liver sauce. Kakinuma is widely considered the master of sushi in Ginza.

MITSUHIRO ARAKI
The Araki, London, England

Mitsuhiro Araki was raised in Japan on Western-style cuisine cooked by his grandfather, so when he decided to pursue a culinary career after high school, sushi was not his first choice. But after working in two restaurants in Japan, he moved to Australia in 1990 and saw an opportunity to increase global interest in Japanese cuisine, and sushi in particular. Araki became determined to become a master sushi chef. In 2000 he opened his eponymous sushi restaurant in Tokyo's Ginza district. He ran it for twelve years and earned a coveted three-Michelin-star rating, arguably the pinnacle achievement for a Japanese sushi chef. So what do you do when you're at the top of your sushi game at the epicenter of the culinary art form? You shut it down, move to London, and start all over, of course.

In 2014, he opened a ten-seat sushi counter called the Araki that serves an omakase menu for $398 per person and offers only two dinner seatings per night. The restaurant earned two Michelin stars in 2015 and three Michelin stars in 2018. No longer sourcing ingredients from Tokyo's Tsukiji fish market, Araki depends on local fish and produce. He creates dishes that combine the tradition of Japanese sushi with other cuisines, such as mixed Irish tuna with Italian truffles, or New Zealand king salmon topped with Almas caviar. As one of a handful of chefs who have achieved the three-Michelin-star distinction, and the first to do so at a Japanese restaurant in the UK, Araki is widely considered the best master chef in Europe.

Araki has announced that he will hand off the Araki to his sous chef, Marty Lau, and return to Japan. The sushi world looks forward to the next chapter for this famed chef who has committed himself to sharing the world of Japanese sushi with people of all cultures.

We would be remiss if we failed to mention the creative genius of Nobu Matsuhisa, who began his career as a chef and now is chiefly a restaurateur. Although he is best known for his trendy, upscale Nobu restaurant chain, he comes from humble beginnings in 1940s Japan. He is a pioneer in the overall global success of Japanese cuisine and has championed a fusion of Peruvian fare with traditional sushi; his influence on dining culture cannot be overstated. If you've ever enjoyed yellowtail in ponzu sauce, sushi topped with mango, or black cod with miso sauce, you have him to thank.

SUSHI
AT
HOME

EQUIPMENT FOR MAKING YOUR OWN SUSHI

If you're interested in making and serving sushi at home, we advise you to think of it more like a hobby than a one-off activity. From cooking rice perfectly to slicing fish like a pro, you'll likely need time and practice to get things right. The upside is that once you master the basics, you can experiment with different ingredients and techniques. As with most hobbies, you'll want to invest in some essential equipment. Most of the items below are available in specialty cookware or restaurant-supply stores, Asian markets, or major online retailers.

- **Knives:** It's imperative that you have at least one good-quality sharp knife that can easily slice through fish, vegetables, and sushi rolls without sawing or hacking. We recommend stocking up on an 8- or 10-inch chef's knife; a fish knife with a long, slim blade; and a vegetable knife for peeling, slicing, and chopping.

- **Rice cooker:** Cooking sushi rice in a pot on the stove requires attention to make sure the water doesn't boil over and that the rice doesn't burn before it's cooked. This handy appliance is nearly foolproof for making perfectly cooked rice and frees you up to perform other prep work.

- **Bamboo rolling mat:** This tool is indispensable for forming tight maki rolls. Different sizes are available; anything larger than 8 inches by 7 inches (the size of most nori sheets) will work.

- **Plastic wrap:** Keep this common kitchen storage material on hand for preventing rice from sticking to your rolling mat.

- **Large wooden bowl** for mixing and serving large batches of rice (such as for a sushi party; see page 133)

- **Sheet pan** for cooking sushi rice

- **Rice paddle or wooden spoon** for seasoning rice

- **Small bowls and plates** for storing ingredients

- **Cutting board**

- **Fine-mesh strainer** for washing rice and vegetables

- **Dish towel** to clean and dry hands and utensils

BUILDING YOUR SUSHI SHOPPING LIST

You can incorporate any number of ingredients in your sushi; think of this list as a good starting point that covers the basic needs. Many items will be available at your local supermarket, whereas some may require a visit to an Asian market, specialty grocer, or online retailer.

- **Fish:** Salmon and tuna tend to be the most popular and most readily available. (See page 114 for tips on selecting sushi-grade fish.)

- **Sushi rice:** You want short-grained white rice with the term *sushi rice* right on the label. This kind of rice is more absorbent than other varieties, which means it will be stickier and hold together well in nigiri and maki rolls.

- **Vegetables:** Avocado, cucumber, asparagus, sweet potato, and shiitake mushrooms are popular, but anything that can be cut into thin strips or easily rolled, such as leafy vegetables, is a good option.

- **Nori:** These thin sheets of pressed dried seaweed are essential for hand rolls and maki. They are sold in most supermarkets in 8-inch-by-7-inch rectangles. Store leftover nori in a resealable container or bag to keep out moisture and prevent the sheets from softening.

- **Japanese rice vinegar:** Made from fermented rice, this vinegar has a slightly sweet flavor and is the key to making perfectly seasoned sushi rice. It's also a welcome addition to salad dressings and marinades.

- **Granulated sugar** for seasoning sushi rice

- **Wasabi:** Some sushi recipes call for wasabi as an ingredient, and you'll want it on hand to mix into soy sauce. It is sold in different forms; for simplicity and ease, consider purchasing it as a paste.

- **Pickled ginger** as a palate cleanser and garnish

- **Soy sauce:** we recommend *koikuchi*, or dark, soy sauce (see page 59 for more)

- **Kewpie Japanese mayonnaise** for topping maki rolls or mixing with sriracha to make a spicy mayo. It's even great on a sandwich! But note that it contains MSG.

- **Toasted sesame seeds** for inside-out rolls

HOW TO SELECT AND STORE SUSHI-GRADE FISH

The terms *sushi grade* and *sashimi grade* are marketing buzzwords used by sales teams in order to expand raw fish consumption beyond Japanese restaurants, where many patrons inherently trust that uncooked fish is safe for consumption. No governing body grades fish freshness, though some, such as the U.S. Food and Drug Administration (FDA), issue advisory guides on handling and preparing. Ultimately, sellers determine whether fish may be designated as sushi grade and is safe to eat raw.

To be sure that the fish you're buying is suitable for sushi, get to know your local fishmonger. Ask plenty of questions about the best fish to use for sushi as well as how the seller selects and stores products. Freezing fish (preferably as soon as it is caught) for 15 hours kills parasites, and filleting at the market reduces the chance of improper handling. Frequent shipments to the market are another indicator of likely freshness and safety.

Keep in mind that some types of fish are easier to procure in certain areas and during certain seasons.

A good supplier will understand the seasonality and variety available for your locale, so inquire about these details as well. And keep in mind the following information when faced with the fish.

HOW TO SELECT WHOLE FISH

Presentation: The fish should be buried in ice and positioned as it would be if swimming through the water. This orientation prevents gravity from altering the fish's structure (organs, skin, etc.) and, as a result, diminishing the quality.

Eyes: The eyes should be clear, wet, and shiny. Cloudy eyes indicate a fish that is past its prime.

Fins: The tail and dorsal fins should be full, wet, and thick. Avoid torn, dry, or brittle fins.

Flesh: The flesh should appear plump and full, rather than sunken or dry. When touched, it should spring back into position (like your own skin). It should also feel wet, cold, and slick.

Gills: The gills should be bright red.

Scales: The scales should be shiny and firm.

Smell: All fish will have an aroma that is, well, fishy. But if a fish gives off a strong and unpleasant odor, put it back.

Note that whole fish will need to be scaled, gutted, and filleted before you can make sushi or sashimi. If you're not sure how to do this process your fishmonger can likely do it for you at the market. Or you can purchase fish that's already been filleted (see below).

HOW TO SELECT PACKAGED FILLETED FISH

No cracks or breaks: The white lines running through the fillet are collagen sheaths. Avoid fish showing separation between collagen sheaths, which may indicate that the fillet has been mishandled or the collagen has started to break down.

No pooled water in the package: This usually indicates that the fish is no longer retaining moisture because it has sat for too long.

Appearance: Generally, the fish should be wet and glossy. White fish should be translucent. Darker fish should be saturated in color.

Once you purchase either whole or filleted fish, store it in the refrigerator and aim to use it within twenty-four hours of purchase to ensure that it stays fresh and clean from bacteria. Only freeze fish that hasn't already been frozen and thawed, and when you're ready to thaw it, do so in the refrigerator, not at room temperature.

TIP: Still not sure about shopping for your own fish? Try asking your local sushi restaurant. Some chefs supply patrons with fish for their own use from time to time. Of course, we do not recommended that you request this every week, only on occasion. You will likely pay a premium for the fish, but you will be confident in the quality. Simply ask the chef to order a little extra of the fish you want with the next order for the restaurant.

HOW TO COOK RICE LIKE A SUSHI CHEF

Traditional sushi chefs spend years practicing and perfecting the art of making sushi rice. It's a simple process that takes time to master in order to create the right balance of consistency, texture, and flavor. Following is a basic recipe. Over time, you may want to customize the ingredients to create your own signature sushi rice. Always start with short-grain white rice specifically labeled as "sushi rice," and for best results use a rice cooker, rather than a pot on the stove.

This recipe yields about 4 cups cooked rice, enough for 9 maki rolls or about 24 pieces of nigiri.

WHAT YOU'LL NEED

    3 cups uncooked short-grain sushi rice
    3 cups water, plus more for rinsing rice
    ½ cup rice vinegar
    2 tablespoons granulated sugar
    2 teaspoons fine salt

1. **Wash the rice:** A proper cleaning ensures that your rice is not sticky or smelly. Place the sushi rice in a large bowl and fill with enough cold

water to cover rice by one inch. Swirl your fingers in the water in a circular motion; the water will turn cloudy. Drain the water through a strainer and repeat the washing process as many times as necessary until the water is barely cloudy when you swirl it. A good rule of thumb is to wash once for each cup of rice you are using.

2. **Cook the rice:** Pour the washed rice and 3 cups of fresh water into the rice cooker. Cook according to the manufacturer's instructions.

3. **Prepare the seasoning mixture:** Combine the rice vinegar, sugar, and salt in a small saucepan. Cook over low heat, stirring occasionally, until the sugar dissolves. Let the mixture cool. (Note: With time, you may want to add more or less vinegar to make the rice sweeter.)

4. **Spread the rice:** While the rice is still hot, transfer it to a large sheet pan and spread it into a even layer.

5. **Season the rice:** Sprinkle the vinegar mixture a little at a time over the rice, using a spoon and drizzling in alternating horizontal and vertical motions. Don't pour all the liquid at once because it will cause the rice to clump; try to distribute

it evenly. When done properly, the rice will be sticky, shiny, and slightly cooled. Use the sushi rice right away in your favorite recipe (see pages 123–132).

TIP: Different brands of rice vinegar have varying strengths of flavor. If you are concerned about overseasoning your rice, set aside half of the vinegar mixture. Sprinkle the rest over your rice, and then taste it. Continue adding the mixture until you achieve the desired intensity. Avoid "seasoned" rice vinegar for this recipe, which already has sugar added. Using unseasoned allows you to control the sweetness of your rice.

HOW TO SLICE FISH

Knowing how to slice fish is essential for making beautiful sushi and sashimi at home. As with all aspects of sushi making, this technique takes time to master. Be patient and don't be hard on yourself if you don't nail it on your first try. No matter what, you'll still have a delicious meal.

Fresh raw fish is delicate, so you'll need a razor-sharp knife in order to make smooth, clean cuts without sawing or hacking. Use fish immediately after slicing.

MAKI

Practice this technique first if you're a total beginner. Because the fish will be rolled inside the rice and seaweed, maki is forgiving of less-than-stellar cuts. Place the fillet on a cutting board. Slice the fish parallel to the longer side of the fillet, drawing the knife into the flesh at an angle to the strands of connective tissue, to create long strips that are almost boxlike in shape and about ½ inch wide.

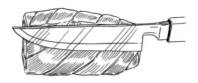

SASHIMI AND CHIRASHI

Place the fillet on the cutting board. Slice into the fillet with the knife parallel to the shorter side, creating slices about 1 centimeter thick.

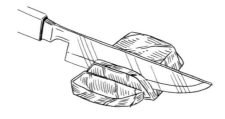

NIGIRI

Place the fillet on a cutting board. Hold your knife at a 45-degree angle about an inch from one corner near the shorter side. Slice diagonally across and down to the corner, increasing the angle of the knife slightly, to make a concave slice. If cutting a fish with collagen sheaths, hold your knife so that the blade is perpendicular to the sheaths.

HOW TO ROLL MAKI

Maki rolls are endlessly versatile. Raw fish, cooked beef, crisp fresh vegetables—the options are limited only by your imagination (or maybe what's currently in your refrigerator!). See page 127 for suggested fillings, or experiment with ingredients to create your own signature roll. The instructions below call for a full sheet of nori; we recommend that beginners use a full sheet to avoid overstuffing, which will prevent the roll from holding together. As you master this skill, you may find that a half sheet is enough.

WHAT YOU'LL NEED

1 sheet nori (roughly 8 inches by 7 inches)

1 cup water

2 tablespoons rice vinegar

1 cup cooked sushi rice (see page 118)

1 to 3 strips sliced fish (see page 121),
    or to taste

2 to 4 strips sliced vegetables, or to taste

Sauces for filling or topping, such as spicy
    mayonnaise or eel sauce

Soy sauce

Wasabi

Pickled ginger

1. **Prepare your bamboo mat:**
Wrap the mat in plastic wrap
to ensure that the rice does
not stick to it. Place the mat
on a clean work surface and lay
the nori on it with the rough side facing up.
Position the nori about two inches from the bottom of the mat.

2. **Wet your fingers:** In a small bowl,
combine the water and rice vinegar.
Set it next to your bamboo mat.
Lightly moisten your fingers
in the mixture and continue
to do so as you prepare the
sushi regularly to prevent the
rice from sticking to your hands.

3. **Spread the rice:** Gently
press a small handful
(about the size of a ten-
nis ball) of cooked sushi rice
onto the nori and spread it evenly across the sheet
to all the edges but one, leaving about 1 inch of
the top edge uncovered so that you can seal the
roll.

TIP: To make *uramaki*, or an inside-out roll, gently flip the rice and nori together so that the rice is on the bottom and the nori is on top. Proceed with instructions and, if desired, drizzle the outside with your favorite sauce before slicing and serving.

4. **Layer your fillings:** Place the sliced fish and vegetable fillings across the center of the nori on top of the rice. Add sauces, if using.

5. **Time to roll:** Carefully lift the bottom edge of the bamboo mat with your thumbs and gently hold the fillings in place with your fingertips as you roll the mat over the fillings. Roll while pressing the fillings until you feel the bottom edge of the nori touch your fingertips. Pull the bamboo mat toward you a bit, then press the roll gently to keep it tight. Repeat the rolling motion, lifting with your thumbs while pressing with your fingertips and pulling the mat a bit closer after each roll.

Roll as tightly and evenly as possible, moistening your fingertips as necessary to prevent sticking.

6. **Seal the roll:** Lift the bamboo mat. Use a moistened fingertip to dab a bit of water-vinegar mixture on the top edge of the nori and press it into the roll to seal. Refrigerate for 10 minutes.

7. **Cut the roll:** Place the long roll on a cutting board. Using a sharp, slightly moistened knife, slice the roll into 8 equal pieces, wiping the blade with a dish towel between cutes, Alternatively, slice the roll in half, then line up the halves and halve them; line up the quarters, and cut in half once more. Remember to wipe the blade to prevent sticking.

8. **Serve:** Serve your maki rolls with soy sauce, wasabi, and ginger.

FILLING COMBINATIONS

Use your favorite ingredients or try these popular combinations.

California roll: Imitation crab stick, sliced avocado, strips of cucumber, and sesame seeds to sprinkle on top (make this one inside out)

Philadelphia roll: Strips of salmon (fresh or smoked), strips of cucumber, and a bit of cream cheese

Spicy tuna roll: Diced tuna tossed with a mixture of Kewpie Japanese mayonnaise and chili sauce either inside the roll or piled on top

Mixed vegetable roll: Strips of cucumber and carrot, scallions, sliced avocado, asparagus spears, and a bit of cream cheese

Surf-and-turf roll: Imitation crab stick, cooked beef, sliced avocado, and strips of cucumber, carrot, tuna, and salmon

HOW TO SHAPE NIGIRI

Nigiri is the most traditional style of sushi. The technique for slicing fish for this style is a bit more advanced than for maki, sashimi, and chirashi (see page 121), and forming the rice can be challenging at first. But once you master it, you're sure to impress friends and family with these elegant little morsels. The following recipe makes about 6 to 8 nigiri.

WHAT YOU'LL NEED

1 cup water
2 tablespoons rice vinegar
1 cup cooked sushi rice (see page 118)
Wasabi for shaping nigiri, plus more for serving
About 6 to 8 slices of fish (see page 121)
Soy sauce
Pickled ginger

1. **Prepare your work station:** On a clean surface, set out a small bowl, a large serving plate, and all your ingredients.

2. **Wet your hands:** In the small bowl, combine the water and rice vinegar. Lightly moisten your palms and fin-  gertips to prevent the sushi rice from sticking. Keep the bowl handy and remoisten as needed.

3. **Shape the rice:** Mold a ping-pong-ball-sized portion of rice into an oval. Cup it in one hand where your fingers meet your palm and hold it in place with your thumb. With the  thumb and middle finger of your other hand, press the sides of the rice to form a loose rectangular box. Grasp the short ends with your thumb and fingertips and rotate it 180 degrees. Cup and press as before, then flip it over. Continue cupping, pressing, rotating, and flipping until the rice is firm and hold its shape. Place on the plate.

4. **Assemble:** Place one slice of fish in your hand at the base of your fin- gers. Dab a little wasabi onto the center of the fish, which will help it stick to the rice. Place the formed

rice on top of the fish and gently press to adhere the fish to the rice.

5. **Reshape:** Flip the assembled nigiri and place it fish side up at the base of your fingers. Repeat the pressing and rotating steps you used to mold the rice until the nigiri is perfectly formed and the fish is held firmly in place.

6. **Serve:** Place formed nigiri on the serving plate. Serve with additional wasabi, soy sauce, and pickled ginger.

HOW TO BUILD A CHIRASHI BOWL

A chirashi bowl is the easiest kind of sushi to make at home. It consists of a mound of sushi rice topped with fish, vegetables, and other ingredients. It's a versatile dish that's a cinch to prepare and makes a great customizable option to serve when hosting a group that includes vegetarians. (For more tips on throwing a sushi party at home, see page 133.) The following recipe makes one chirashi bowl.

WHAT YOU'LL NEED

1½ cups freshly cooked sushi rice
  (see page 118)

½ cup mixed chilled fish such as raw tuna, raw salmon, or raw yellowtail, sliced ¼ inch thick

3 tablespoons salmon roe

½ ounce each thinly sliced vegetables of your choice, such as avocado, poached asparagus, scallions, radishes, cucumbers, or shiitake mushrooms

Optional: pickled ginger and/or soy sauce, for serving

Place the sushi rice at the bottom of a serving bowl. Spread the seafood, salmon roe, vegetables, and any other desired toppings over the rice. (For a more eye-catching presentation, add each topping one at a time, creating small piles on the rice.) Eat immediately, served with pickled ginger and soy sauce as desired.

HOW TO THROW A SUSHI PARTY

Making sushi can be a fun dinner party activity that allows for taste experimentation while catering to beginners and experienced sushi lovers alike. And after perfecting your own sushi rice (page 118), maki (page 123), and nigiri (page 128), a sushi party is a great opportunity for showing off your skills and teaching friends how to make their own creations.

We recommend first-time party hosts plan a menu in advance—California rolls, mixed vegetable rolls, tuna rolls, and salmon rolls are good options—and purchase ingredients specifically for those rolls. With experience, you may stock up on a variety of ingredients and experiment with different combinations, then vote on whose roll is the tastiest. Make sure you've got all the essential equipment (see page 110) for guests to use and plenty of serve ware, like small plates, soy sauce holders, large platters, chopsticks, and small bowls for prepped ingredients. Think about what other foods, beverages, and/or desserts will round out the meal, such as miso soup, seaweed salad, gyoza, edamame, sake, green tea, and mochi ice cream balls, and stock up in advance.

PARTY PREP

On the day of the party, take care of this prep work up to 4 hours before guests arrive.

Make the rice: Cook about 1 cup of rice for each party guest, which is enough for 3 rolls per person. (See page 118 for instructions.) Cover and let stand at room temperature.

Select, clean, and slice the fillings: Offer a mix of fish and vegetables. Chill in airtight containers until party time.

Set up work stations with the following items:

- **Small bowls for dipping hands:** Offer a mixture of 1 cup of water and 2 tablespoons of rice vinegar for guests to dip their hands into while making sushi to prevent the rice from sticking.

- **Nori:** Keep full 8-by-7-inch sheets dry in sealed containers.

- **Bamboo mats:** If you don't have enough for each guest, you can use sheets of plastic wrap cut slightly larger than your nori sheets.

- **A cutting board and a sharp knife:** Set up a single maki-slicing station. For safety, and if children will be present, it's a good idea to have just one sharp knife to keep track of.

- **Condiments:** Offer individual bowls of soy sauce, pickled ginger, and wasabi. If using ponzu sauce or spicy mayonnaise, present these in squeeze bottles or small bowls with spoons.

Just prior to the start of the party, set out your prepped fresh ingredients. Pile sushi rice into a large wooden bowl and present sliced fish and vegetables in small serving bowls (or pack fish in crushed ice).

PARTY TIME!

By now all the prep work is done, you're surely a master of making sushi (thanks to the instructions on pages 118–132), and it's time to pass the knowledge on to your friends. Demonstrate how to assemble maki rolls or a chirashi bowl using the ingredients and materials presented, and then invite guests to make their own. Or for a more cooperative style, break into pairs, couples, or small groups to divide and conquer the process. Have any appetizers or finger foods ready as soon as people arrive so they aren't ravenous while they learn a new skill. And remember: practice makes perfect, and even a misshapen maki will taste delicious.

SAKE OPTIONS

If the crowd is right, you can round out the party experience by including sake (see page 95 for more information).

BYO: Offer your favorite sake and encourage guests to bring their own. Take time to sample the different kinds. Provide "tasting notes" cards for guests to record their observations about each sample, then compare reactions.

Sake flights: Purchase four different sakes, one of each of the main categories, that meet your budget. Mix flavors and temperatures to your liking. Then prepare flights for guests to sample all four at once. Typically, sake is served in 4- to 6-ounce pours in tiny porcelain cups called *o-chokos*. It may be complicated (and expensive) to serve in this manner, so consider using small plastic cups (it's a party, after all) or pouring one sake at a time. Either way, encourage your guests to enjoy each sample at roughly the same time to allow for social discussion.

Blind sake tasting: This variation requires an investment but can lead to a big win for one guest. Encourage each guest or couple to bring two bottles of the same sake wrapped in wrapping paper—but in a way that allows for the bottle to be opened without removing the paper. Upon arrival, one bottle should be placed in an area marked "To Be Tasted" and labeled with a letter (A, B, C, etc.) and the other in an area marked "The Prize." Provide each guest with a sheet of paper listing all the letters. Ask them to sample each sake throughout the night and then rank them in order from most to least favorite. Collect the completed sheets and add up the scores for each letter. The letter/ bottle with the lowest score wins the taste test. And the person who brought that bottle wins all the "Prize" bottles. Alternatively, you can ask guests to bring one bottle and offer something else as the prize (perhaps a copy of this book!).

Sake bombs: This drink consists of a shot glass of sake that is dropped (or poured) into a pint of beer and then chugged. The sake and beer are up to you; we suggest opting for a Japanese beer. To make things extra-interesting, try placing two parallel chopsticks on top of the beer-filled pint glass (spaced almost as far apart as the diameter of the shot glass) and resting the shot glass of sake on top of the chopsticks. Bang your fists on the table, causing the shot glass to drop into the pint. The drinker should chug immediately. This is especially fun if you have a group of drinkers lined up around the table and everyone bangs on the table to the count of three or, in Japanese: "ichi," "ni," "san," *bang!*

OTHER BEVERAGES

Cocktails and Japanese beer can pair well with sushi too, and don't forget about Japanese green tea, especially for guests who don't drink alcohol. Avoid overly sweet cocktails, which generally don't pair well with fish. We recommend the following.

Sake mojito (or another sake-infused cocktail): Replace the rum with sake in this fresh, minty drink.

Margarita: The salted rim of this Mexican mainstay matches the salty notes in the rice and fish.

Gin and tonic: The flavors of gin pair well with tuna and salmon.

Vodka martini or Moscow mule: The neutral taste of vodka will keep the flavors of the sushi front and center. Bonus points if you use a Japanese vodka that's distilled from rice.

Champagne: A dry sparkling wine is easy to serve and rich in flavor but won't compete with the sushi.

ENTERTAINMENT

The sushi preparation and eating will fill the bulk of your party. But if you want to include other forms of entertainment, consider these suggestions.

Play games: When the sushi is finished, kick back with a cup of sake and play store-bought games like Sushi Go or Sushi Draft, available online and at some specialty game retailers. Or try our DIY game below.

THE TIC TAC GAME

Provide each guest with a bowl filled with an equal number of Tic Tacs (minimum 15) and a set of fresh chopsticks. When you say go, the race is on to remove every Tic Tac from the bowl using only the chopsticks. The first person to finish wins.

Sushi trivia: This book is full of history, facts, and tips about sushi. Share information throughout the night with guests in conversation, or print facts on note cards and place them at appropriate spots around the party. (For example, you can include information about sake at your sake bar.) Then create a quiz-show-style game later in the evening and award points for correctly answered questions. The person who earns the most points wins.

Invite a professional: You might ask your favorite local sushi restaurant if their chefs are available to give demonstrations for private parties. Although this kind of party likely will cost more than taking a DIY approach, there's nothing like learning how to make sushi from an experienced chef. They can share personal anecdotes and professional knowledge from years behind the sushi bar.

RESOURCES

For further reading about sushi, we recommend *The Sushi Experience* by Hiroko Shimbo. *Sake Confidential: A Beyond-the-Basics Guide to Understanding, Tasting, Selection, and Enjoyment* by John Gauntner is another excellent resource.

Websites we recommend include the Sushi Geek (thesushigeek.com) and Sushi FAQ (sushifaq.com).

When you're ready to make your own sushi, check out MTC Kitchen (mtckitchen.com/sushi-supplies). The online store of this Manhattan restaurant supplier sells everything you could want for making, eating, and sharing sushi at home, from bamboo rolling mats, sushi knives, and rice cookers to serving dishes and rice presses and molds.

ACKNOWLEDGMENTS

A huge thank-you to our friends Nick, Peter, Cindy, Marina, and the entire Ota-Ya family in Newtown, Pennsylvania, and Lambertville, New Jersey. You always welcome us with a smile and something new to try and truly foster our love for sushi. Your time, knowledge, anecdotes, and demonstrations enriched the writing experience and added valuable information to this book.

Thank you to Jhanteigh and Jane for your insightful guidance in putting this book together. Thank you to Elissa for that amazing cover and Molly for overall design work. Thank you to John and the production team, Nicole and the marketing team, and Moneka and the sales team for delivering this book into the world. And thanks to the entire Quirk team for all you do every day for this book and others.

Thank you to our family and friends for joining us on this adventure. And for allowing us to order way too much sushi—yet somehow always finishing it with us.

ABOUT THE AUTHORS

MARC LUBER has been enamored of all things sushi since he tried his first spicy scallop hand roll twenty years ago. He is the author of *Stuff Every Cannabisseur Should Know* and lives with his family outside Philadelphia, Pennsylvania.

BRETT COHEN enjoys fresh *tako* sashimi, opts for the shrimp tempura roll, and prefers his sake chilled. He is the author of *Stuff Every Man Should Know* and *Stuff Every Dad Should Know* and a coauthor of *Recipes Every Man Should Know*. He lives outside Philadelphia, Pennsylvania.